ORANGE COIN GOOD

ORANGE COIN GOOD

THE VALUE OF BITCOIN
BOOK ONE

jimbo

October 26, 2020

v1.0.3

Bitcoin Citadel Press

To my Grandma, for always listening.

CONTENTS

Preface

"Any technology that is going to have significant impact in the next 10 years is already at least 10 years old. Any technology that is going to have significant impact in the next 5 years is already at least 15 years old, and likely still below the radar. Hence, beware of anyone arguing for some 'new' idea that is 'going to' take off in the next 5 years, unless they can trace its history back for 15."

—*Bill Buxton*[1]

On January 3, 2019, the Bitcoin blockchain turned 10 years old. The world is not ready for Bitcoin, Bitcoin is not ready for the world, and yet, here it is.

The question at the heart of this book series is "What is the Value of Bitcoin?" If you've heard of Bitcoin and are looking to understand why people are excited about it and what it means for the future, then this series is for you.

Please note that this series is about Bitcoin specifically, not the concept of cryptocurrencies, digital assets or blockchain technology in general. Throughout this series, Bitcoin refers to the project described in Satoshi Nakamoto's 2008 white paper[2] and its blockchain-based ledger started on January 3, 2009[3].

For better or worse, because the Bitcoin software is Open Source, it's relatively easy for anyone with the technical know-how to spin up a project that meets these criteria and to call it 'Bitcoin'. And since the Bitcoin name and logo are in the public domain[4][5], there is no individual or corporation that can claim ownership over it.

This can be confusing for newcomers who are trying to ascertain which is the 'real' Bitcoin. Fret not. We'll talk more about what distinguishes consensus Bitcoin from its various clones and forks in the second book of this series. For now, suffice it to say that consensus Bitcoin is that which the consensus of participants agrees it to be. If a given project has to change its name in order to distinguish itself from consensus Bitcoin (for example by adding a suffix), then it is not the subject of this book series.

Who Should Read This Book?

This book is for Precoiners. In Bitcoin parlance, a Precoiner is someone who has not yet made up their mind about Bitcoin. If you are a Precoiner who is open to learning about the Value of Bitcoin, then this book is for you.

In contrast to Precoiners, a Nocoiner is someone who has made up their mind against Bitcoin. This could be for a variety of reasons, many of which are misconceptions that we'll discuss throughout this series. If you are a Nocoiner who's decidedly against Bitcoin, you're welcome to read on, but this book will probably not persuade you.

If you are already a Bitcoiner, then this book contains mostly stuff you already know. I would greatly appreciate your feedback (especially if I got something wrong). But this book is designed for your Precoiner friends and loved ones. Consider giving them a copy.

What's in This Series?

The question of the Value of Bitcoin is a complex one, because coming to an answer requires insights from different disciplines. Bitcoin sits at the nexus of diverse areas of study, including technology (of course), but also game theory, psychology, philosophy, economics, law, finance, and the list goes on.

In short, the thesis of this series is that at saturation, Bitcoin will emerge as the de facto global metric of intersubjective value. Put bluntly, any value that can be measured in Bitcoin will come to be measured in Bitcoin.

This is a maximally bullish claim, and I don't expect you to accept it without justification. The motto of the

Bitcoin community is "don't trust, verify." And so I implore you to do your own research (DYOR) and come to your own conclusions.

Having said that, each book in this series deals with a specific sub-question. Together, the answers to these questions build towards a complete explanation of the Value of Bitcoin. In order, these questions are:

1. How can a purely digital money that's not backed by anything have any value at all?

2. Even if Bitcoin has value to some people, how can you be sure that it won't just disappear or become supplanted by something else?

3. Supposing that Bitcoin manages to survive, how much could it be worth in the long term (the lowercase 'v' value of Bitcoin)?

4. What will be the far reaching effects of Bitcoin on the future organization of human affairs (the capital 'V' Value of Bitcoin)?

By their nature, these questions are increasingly speculative. This book deals only with the first. The following section describes the chapters of this book and what you'll find in them.

What's in This Book?

This book answers the question, "how can a purely digital money that's not backed by anything have any value at all?" Here's a brief description of what you'll find in each part and chapter.

Part I

Why do we need Bitcoin?

Chapter 1 — Green Paper Bad

In this chapter we'll discuss the current dominant monetary regime, fiat currency. You'll learn how central banks create price inflation intentionally to siphon away your purchasing power. You'll see how that lost value is transferred to the State, the banks and the wealthy. We'll also discuss how fiat currency is responsible for the boom-bust cycle and how it perpetuates debt culture. We need good money, and Bitcoin fixes this.

Chapter 2 — Because We Need Good Money

Why Bitcoin? Cooperation is widespread in nature, but humans have a superlative ability to cooperate and co-ordinate across time and distance. In this chapter, we'll dig into the fundamental human characteristics that give rise to our need for good money. Specifically we'll talk about reciprocity and how we detect and deter cheaters. You'll see how ledgers and money are technologies that enable large scale cooperation and facilitate human flourishing. With this framing in place, we'll be ready to dive into the inverted world of Bitcoin.

Chapter 3 — Down the Rabbit Hole

Having established our need for good money, and how fiat currency fails to satisfy this need, it's time to introduce Bitcoin. You'll learn that Bitcoin is three things: programmable money, a computer network, and a social phenomenon. These three parts—the social, the technological and the monetary—are mutually reinforcing, governed by consensus, and inseparable.

Expanding on those definitions, we'll chart a conceptual map of the territory including Bitcoin and the environment that it inhabits. You'll get a 50,000 foot view of the complex and interconnected landscape adjoining Bitcoin to the outside world.

Chapter 4 — Meeting the People of Bitcoin

In this chapter you'll learn about Bitcoiners—the people of Bitcoin. Specifically, we'll discuss HODLers (HODL is an intentional misspelling of 'hold'), researchers, developers and miners. You'll also learn the roles that merchants and traders play in price discovery (monetary consensus). Although these groups have different and sometimes conflicting goals, together they provide an interdependent social network that imbues the Bitcoin monetary units and computer network with value.

Part II

How does Bitcoin work (for you)?

Chapter 5 — Setting Up Your First Wallet

When you have some Bitcoin, what you really have is the ability to transfer amounts that are encoded in the Bitcoin blockchain. Your wallet is a piece of software that helps you view your balance and initiate transactions. It's similar to how your web browser is software that lets you view and interact with web pages on the Internet. In this chapter, you'll learn the three steps to setting up your first Bitcoin wallet.

Chapter 6 — Receiving Your First Bitcoin

With your wallet ready, in this chapter we'll walk through the six steps to receive amounts of Bitcoin with it. You'll see how each step has a similar counterpart for receiving an email. This may seem complex, probably harder than it is. But this is because the user interface to Bitcoin hasn't caught up to the technological possibilities. It took many years for email to transform from an arcane technology to a tap-and-swipe operation on a smartphone. So it is with Bitcoin.

Chapter 7 — Securing Your Bitcoin

While the previous chapter was about how to receive Bitcoin, this chapter focuses on how to secure it. You'll learn about the different kinds of wallets and what trade-offs they incur. We'll discuss the concept of a hot wallet and a cold wallet. By the end, you should know how to choose among the different kinds of wallets to store different amounts of value to you.

Part III

What does Bitcoin achieve?

Chapter 8 — Digital Rivalry and Excludability

Now that you've seen how Bitcoin works for you, let's talk about what Bitcoin achieves. To be good money, a monetary media needs to be four things: rival, excludable, fungible and hard. In this chapter, we'll discuss the first two. You'll see how Bitcoin gave birth to digital rivalry. All prior digital goods were merely promises, but Bitcoin is the thing itself. After that, we'll talk about excludability—the property that makes ownership possible. You'll learn how Bitcoin is superior to both gold and fiat currency in terms of rivalry and excludability.

Chapter 9 — Fungibility and Hardness

Continuing our discussion of the monetary properties of Bitcoin, in this chapter we'll discuss fungibility and hardness. Fungibility has to do with the degree to which monetary units are interchangeable. You'll see how Bitcoin is mostly fungible and how that situation is improving over time. You'll learn how fiat currency and gold stack up in regard to fungibility. With regards to hardness, nothing competes with Bitcoin. It is the hardest money ever conceived. This has profound implications for its ability to satisfy our inherent need for reciprocity.

Chapter 10 — Metric of Intersubjective Value

In this final chapter, we'll depart from simply describing the status quo and project forward into the future. First, we'll discuss the different kinds of things people buy and how we measure their value today. You'll see that different value metrics are used in different contexts. Then we'll speculate as to the role Bitcoin will play in the future at saturation—that is, when everyone groks the Value of Bitcoin. I predict that Bitcoin will arise as the global standard of measure for expressing intersubjective value. Anything that can be measured in Bitcoin will come to be measured in Bitcoin. We close with a look to the road ahead.

What This Book is Not

Bitcoin is a transformational technology that you can look at and study from many different angles. One book cannot cover all of them. Here are some topics this book will explicitly not cover.

Technical Manual

This is not a technical manual on the inner workings of Bitcoin or blockchain. If you're looking for the nitty-gritty details about the mathematics and protocols that power Bitcoin, read *Mastering Bitcoin* by Andreas Antonopoulos[6].

How to Buy

This book is not a complete user's manual for Bitcoin. Although we'll discuss a few of the details about how Bitcoin is stored and transferred, this book will not go into great detail on where or how to buy Bitcoin. It's important to Do Your Own Research (DYOR) when it comes to choosing Bitcoin exchanges and wallet software.

Financial or Trading Advice

Traders actively buy and sell Bitcoin and other assets to try to eke out a profit when the price fluctuates. This book will define some of the lingo that crypto traders and enthusiasts use, but DO NOT interpret this as trading advice. You are responsible for your own finances.

Legal or Tax Advice

The regulatory environment around Bitcoin is complex and evolving. DO NOT take this as legal or tax advice. Each jurisdiction has its nuances. You are responsible for your own legal and tax liabilities.

With that preamble out of the way, let's dive into the inverted world of Bitcoin.

PART I

Why do we need Bitcoin?

CHAPTER 1
Green Paper Bad

The meme "Green Paper Bad" is shorthand for a profound truth. The currency that we use is bad, and everyone knows it—at least on a subconscious level.

By "currency" here, I don't mean money in general, although people sometimes use those terms interchangeably. I mean, specifically, sovereign currency, also known as fiat currency (or just "fiat"). Fiat currency consists of the bills and coins issued by a nation state or a supranational organization, and bank account values denominated in same[7]. All of it is "green paper", and it's all bad.

The evidence that green paper is bad is all around us. Consider: suppose you had a windfall of money, enough to pay off your debts with some left over. What would you do with the surplus? Would you keep physical bills stuffed under your mattress? Would you keep it in a bank account?

Most people with extra money would not stuff it in the mattress or leave it in the bank, and for good reason. The value of fiat currency is continuously reduced over time due to a phenomenon that economists call *inflation*. When the prices of things go up, it means the value of your money has gone down. Because of price inflation—increase in prices denominated in fiat—

people are motivated to get rid of their money in either of two ways: spend it or invest it. This is on purpose, and it's bad for you.

Every modern fiat currency is managed by a central bank. In the United States, the central bank is the Federal Reserve System (Fed for short). In the Eurozone, it's the European Central Bank (ECB). There's the People's Bank of China (PBOC), the Reserve Bank of India (RBI), and so on.

While the various central banks have different mandates from their countries' legislatures, they have many features in common. Chief among them is the goal of price stability, which most central banks interpret as low, stable inflation. It is the expressed goal of many central banks to generate 2% price inflation annually[8][9], but it can be even higher[10].

If your central bank achieves its stated goal, your money will be worth 2% less next year than it is now, 2% less the year after that, and so on in perpetuity. 2% may not sound like a big number, but the compounded effect is devastating. The following figure shows the purchasing power decline of 2% inflation compared to a fixed tax rate of 20%.

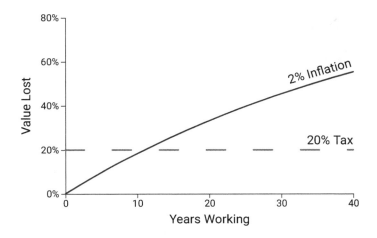

Value lost to 2% inflation vs. constant 20% tax rate.

For the first decade, the impact of purchasing power loss due to inflation is less than the fixed tax rate. But starting in year 11, and for every year after, the inflation costs you more than the tax. After 40 years of working, your inflation loss is equivalent to a 55% tax rate. Over half of your purchasing power will be lost to inflation over your working lifetime.

But where does your purchasing power go? If your purchasing power was reduced, was someone else's increased? The answer is "yes", but the mechanism is convoluted. To understand where your purchasing power goes, we have to look at how your central bank creates price inflation in the first place. Then we can evaluate who benefits from this system.

How the Central Bank Creates Price Inflation

The price of something is the ratio of how much money was spent divided by the quantity of stuff that was sold. Divide how much money was spent by how many units were purchased, and that gives you the unit price.

$$Price = \frac{Money}{Goods}$$

Because this is a fraction, any change to either the numerator (Money) or to the denominator (Goods) will result in a change to the price. To achieve its price inflation target of 2%, your central bank needs to either increase the amount of money spent on goods, or decrease the quantity of goods sold (or both).

Thankfully, decreasing the quantity of goods in the economy is pretty much out of the question. Due to human ingenuity and ongoing progress, more goods in a greater variety and higher quality are being invented and produced all the time[11].

So to achieve its price inflation target, the central bank needs to increase the quantity of money over time. But how?

Most new money enters the system by way of commercial bank loans[12]. There's a popular misconception that when you take out a loan, the bank lends you someone else's money (that is, money that some other depositor put there first). This is not true. When you take out a loan, the bank creates two accounting entries: a credit to your account, and a debt that you owe. The money didn't come from anywhere. The credit and the debt both spring into existence at the same time. Banks literally create money from nothing.

The other way that new money enters the system is through deficit spending on the part of the State (the government). Just like commercial banks create credits and debts for regular folks, the central bank creates credits in exchange for debts from the government. To fund its activities, the State issues bonds (debt), which the central bank buys with new money (credit) that it creates from nothing. When the State spends this money on its programs, that money enters the economy, competes with all other spenders, and increases prices for everyone.

OK, so to achieve its inflation target, your central bank needs to increase the money supply (the numerator in the price ratio). To increase the money supply, the central bank needs to create new credit either directly by buying bonds issued by the State, or indirectly by having commercial banks issue more loans. How does the central bank incentivise people to borrow more?

Here's where interest rates come into play. The degree to which people want to take out loans is influenced by how much the loans cost—that is, the interest rate. All other things being equal, the lower the interest rate, the more attractive it is for potential borrowers to take out loans.

The central bank manages key interest rates to incentivise borrowing to increase the money supply to hit its price inflation target. The end result of all this is that your purchasing power is steadily lost. Price inflation is the razor pendulum. The central bank is at the controls.

Following the Money

We're now in position to find out who benefits from your lost purchasing power due to inflation. In short, it's the State, the banks, and the wealthy. Let's talk about each group in turn and how they profit.

The State

The State—that is, the government—is the primary beneficiary of your purchasing power loss due to price inflation. In the words of one former Fed chair, "The dollars the government spends become purchasing power in the hands of the people who received them."[13].

It's a common misconception to think that tax revenue is used to fund State programs. But just like a commercial bank issues loans based on nothing but the promise to repay (debt), the central bank issues loans to the State based on its promises (bonds). By spending new credit money into existence, the State can fund its programs without having to resort to direct taxation. So why have taxes at all?

For a State that issues its own currency, the purpose of taxation is not to fund State programs, but rather to drive demand for the currency so that the State can spend that currency into existence[14]. As long as some people have to pay taxes denominated in the State's currency, those people will accept it as payment for goods and services. This is a sufficient condition for the State to spend the central bank's credit money into the economy, and thereby transfer your purchasing power to itself.

The Banks

The second beneficiary of your purchasing power loss is the banking sector. Banks are in the privileged position of being able to charge interest on the money that they create from nothing. In exchange for this privilege, they are subject to regulation by the central bank. The commercial banks are the paid deputy enforcers of central bank policy.

The Wealthy

The third group who benefits from the status quo is the wealthy. In pursuit of its 2% price inflation goal, the central bank has to decide which items to include in its price calculation. This gives central bank economists some room to negotiate.

One common metric is the Consumer Price Index (CPI), which gauges "prices paid by urban consumers for a market basket of consumer goods and services"[15]. This is a complex measurement that tries to summarize the costs of everyday living.

But by focusing on the prices of consumables, central bank economists omit the prices of assets such as real estate and equity (stocks). The more wealth one has in these kinds of assets, the smaller (as a proportion) one spends on indexed consumables. For example, someone with 100 times the net worth of an average person probably doesn't eat 100 times the food or get 100 times the haircuts.

As the central bank increases the money supply to effect consumer price inflation, they also increase the relative value (and thus price) of the non-cash, unindexed assets held by the wealthy. Meanwhile, the people with the least wealth see the value of their cash savings decrease relative to the prices of their necessities.

Because of price inflation, the rich get richer and the poor get poorer.

Inflation and Your Wages

You might argue that price inflation doesn't affect you personally because your salary has increased during the same period. And as long as your income increases in step with inflation, you won't be affected.

This thinking is wrong for several reasons. The first is that wages do not respond as readily to increases in the money supply as other goods. As an economist would say, labor prices are "sticky", slow to change. Consequently, the costs of your consumer goods may (and often will) increase in advance of increases to your income[16].

Secondly, price inflation devalues not just your current income, but your previous earnings as well. Even if your salary increased more this year than your costs did, the money you made last year (if you've saved any) is worth less in purchasing power now.

Thirdly, what about retirement? If your retirement income is fixed, as is the case for many retirees, you'll find it to be less and less able to cover your expenses as those expenses increase over time due to price inflation.

Price inflation is bad for you, even if you manage to stay ahead of it.

Incentivising Bad Behavior

On top of being bad for you directly, price inflation incentivises bad behavior. It leads to the misallocation of resources and it perpetuates debt culture. Let's look at each.

Misallocating Resources

The interest rate is the price of borrowing money. Like all prices, it conveys information about supply and demand. When interest rates are high, it that means borrowing is expensive (high demand for funds relative to the supply). Likewise, if interest rates are low, then borrowing is cheap (less demand relative to supply).

But central banks use interest rate targeting to achieve their monetary policy goals. This interference distorts the signal that interest rates would otherwise transmit. Borrowers are mislead to believe that more resources are available than there actually are and so they borrow more than they should.

While the credit money for loans is created by the banks from nothing, the real goods that the borrowers would buy are not. Once the borrowers have the bank credit, they have to buy goods from the market. This increases demand for goods and so increases their prices—the inflation that the central bank was hoping

for. Some borrowers may find that they cannot complete the projects that they'd planned because they can
no longer afford the materials[17].

This is the boom of the boom-bust cycle. By creating
money from nothing, banks depress interest rates. This
causes borrowers to over-invest in projects for which
the real resources are not available[18].

Debt Culture

If interest rates were left alone to find their natural lev-
els, people could make sound choices about how much
to spend, how much to save and how much to invest.

But in an environment of artificially depressed interest rates plus increasing prices, saving behavior is pun-
ished. Would-be savers are driven to seek investments
that will yield returns in excess of inflation just to preserve the value that they've earned. This pushes non-
investors into the investing sphere. People are buying
assets that they don't understand to chase returns that
they shouldn't need.

Folks who don't invest are pressured to spend. Or
worse, to borrow. Because of price inflation, debts denominated in fiat currency become easier to pay off as
the currency devalues. This promotes borrowing to
spend on consumption as well as investments, further-
ing the debt cycle.

Companies are trapped too. Even if a fiscally responsible firm would prefer not to take on debt for funding,

it has to compete in the marketplace with other firms that will do so. The rational thing to do is to take the money and go into debt[19].

Voice and Exit

When people are faced with a deteriorating product, they can use their voice to articulate their dissent, and ultimately, if that doesn't work, they can exit, leaving for a competing product[20]. Currencies are subject to this dynamic too. Where an alternative exists, people will abandon their local currency to store value elsewhere.

Consider the case of Argentina, which has an especially atrocious history of currency devaluation. The Argentine peso has lost so much value in recent decades that it would take trillions of today's pesos to buy the equivalent of one peso from 1970. Argentinians are acutely aware of the destruction to purchasing power caused by price inflation. As such, they exit their own currency and save U.S. dollars, despite currency control laws put in place to stop this behavior[21].

The difference between Argentinian hyperinflation and typical price inflation is a difference of degree only. Price inflation everywhere results in purchasing power transfer from everyday people to the State, the banks and the wealthy. The currency devaluations experienced by Argentinians has forced them to store value elsewhere. For them, U.S. dollars are an expedient alternative.

But Americans, whose native currency is the U.S. dollar, and residents of other nations with relatively strong currencies have fewer opportunities to exit. Some have sought change by exercising political voice.

In the lead up to the 2008 U.S. presidential election, conservative Republican candidate Ron Paul ran on a platform to "End the Fed", meaning to abolish the U.S. central bank. Paul argued that the Federal Reserve System was corrupt, unconstitutional and responsible for the inflationary devaluation of the currency[22].

At the other end of the political spectrum, the Occupy Wall Street movement took shape in the autumn of 2011, when protesters set up camp in New York's Zuccotti Park. Occupiers voiced their dissatisfaction over growing wealth inequality and the lack of repercussions to the bankers at the heart of the global financial crisis[23]. While abolishing the Fed was not a headline issue, anti-Fed sentiment ran deep. Many protesters understood that the central bank's policy of continuing price inflation was the root cause of a cascade of other ills[24].

Opposing fiat currency and price inflation—Green Paper Bad—is not a right-wing or a left-wing issue. It's an articulation of a simple truth. Fiat currency is bad money, and everybody knows it.

Fiat currency is created from nothing in order to transfer your purchasing power to the State, the banks and the wealthy. It causes the boom-bust cycle by depressing interest rates. It punishes savers and perpetuates debt culture. It makes the rich richer and the poor poorer.

We need a money which cannot be debased, a true and unimpeachable vehicle for storing and transferring value across time and space. We need a money that resists capture by special interests, a money that is incorruptible and secure. What we need is good money.

Bitcoin fixes this.

CHAPTER 2

Because We Need Good Money

In the previous chapter we discussed the many ways that fiat currency is bad for you. It should be clear that we need better money. But how can Bitcoin, a purely digital money that's not backed by anything, have value to people at all?

It's a fair question. Critics of Bitcoin are quick to point out that unlike sovereign currency which is backed by an issuing government, or gold which is backed by industrial demand, Bitcoin has little non-monetary use[25].

And they're right. So why Bitcoin?

To understand how Bitcoin can have value to people, it helps to know what problem it solves. In this chapter, we'll discuss the key characteristic of human behavior that gives rise to our need for money at all: protecting reciprocal investment. Our proclivity to not only initiate investment in others but to guard against would-be cheaters is well established in the psychological literature. You'll see how reciprocity undergirds our use of ledgers and money as tools to expand and diffuse cooperation.

From this basis, we'll be ready to trek into the inverted world of Bitcoin in the next chapter. By the end of the book, you'll see how Bitcoin accounts for reciprocity across time and distance better than any other system previously conceived.

Protecting Reciprocal Investment

Money is a technology. It's a tool that helps us communicate, cooperate and coordinate. But from where does our need for this technology arise? Cooperation among and between species is widespread in nature[26], but what makes our (human) cooperation special enough to require facilitation via money?

In 1971, Robert L. Trivers proposed that reciprocal investment could be evolutionarily stable[27]. By this he meant that the proclivity to pay a cost in order for another member of the species to benefit (particularly non-kin) could be in the actor's own best interest. This might seem counterintuitive from a purely selfish point of view. Why should anyone, from a survival-of-the-fittest perspective, go out of their way to help someone else, especially someone with whom they share little genetic heritage?

Trivers' answer was multifaceted, but it came down to a calculus weighing the ratio between the cost paid and the benefit received from the act. If members of a species engage in reciprocal investments in which recipients get more benefits than what givers spend, then on net each participant is better off over time. The investment trait would be selected for and thus reinforced in the population.

Simply put, we're all better off if we're willing to help each other in times of need. The problem, though, is cheating.

Dealing With Cheaters

In an environment where population members are willing to initiate investments in each other, a cheater can gain a disproportionate advantage by choosing not to reciprocate. How do you detect and prevent freeriding?

Because both reciprocal investment and cheating are contextually adaptive traits, humans have developed a complex psychology around them. It's not that people fall neatly into categories like 'honest' and 'dishonest', but rather, they occupy a spectrum that changes based on the circumstances[28]. Myriad factors can increase the prevalence of cheating, such as social acceptability and psychological distance from the infraction. But likewise, factors can also reduce the prevalence of cheating, such as overt monitoring, or merely reminding people of codes of honor[29].

It should be no surprise then that we've both honed an acute sensitivity to cheating and evolved various social strategies for dealing with cheaters. For example, given the choice, people like to have the option to punish cheaters—though we'd prefer not to employ the punishment ourselves[30]. And our guilt over our own transgressions leads us to pursue reparative future acts towards others[31]. By selecting trading partners with good reputations, we ostracize those who continually fail to reciprocate, and so on.

Reciprocity is so deeply embedded in our evolutionary psychology that it appears prominently in Jonathan Haidt and Craig Joseph's Moral Foundations Theory[32]. According to the theory, because these moral foundations appear in diverse human populations, they are likely to be more than merely cultural phenomena. The current list of candidate foundations are:

1. Care/Harm

2. Fairness/Cheating

3. Loyalty/Betrayal

4. Authority/Subversion

5. Sanctity/Degradation and

6. Liberty/Oppression[33].

You can think of these as innate pre-wirings that are present in everyone, and then more or less pronounced based on temperament and cultural influences. Moral foundation #2, Fairness/Cheating, is most closely related to reciprocity.

Reciprocity also makes an appearance in the #1 slot of Robert Cialdini's principles of persuasion[34]. Here's the full list:

1. Reciprocity
2. Scarcity
3. Authority
4. Consistency
5. Liking
6. Consensus.

In his book, *Influence: The Psychology of Persuasion*[35], Cialdini refers to these six exploitable traits as "weapons of influence" because compliance practitioners can use them to such great effect.

Even though Reciprocity gets the top slot in Cialdini's list, other traits correspond to our mechanisms for detecting cheaters and reinforcing reciprocal investment. For example, principle #4, Consistency, takes advantage of our desire to remain internally consistent with past commitments that we've made. Honoring one's commitments is a regulation mechanism that reinforces reciprocal investment. Or, as Trivers noted, Liking—Cialdini's principle #5—is a heuristic which increases investment behavior towards friends. Even principle #6, Consensus, also referred to as Social

Proof, can be seen as a shortcut for interpreting and then applying cultural norms (such as reciprocating favors).

So to sum up, reciprocity is an enabler of cooperation. Our proclivity to engage in and protect reciprocal investment is a key driver of our species' success in collaborating across time and distance. Acts of investment toward us trigger a desire to repay, just as we expect (eventually) to see our acts of investment returned by others. Protecting reciprocal investment is the origin of obligations and of debt.

Expanding Cooperation with Ledgers and Money

When tribes are small, like a family unit or neighborhood, informal accounting of unpaid debts is often sufficient[36]. But as communities grow larger, distances increase, and time-to-repay lengthens, we need better tools to keep track than our fallible memories. This is what ledgers and money are designed to do.

When knowledge exceeds the ability of the human mind to faithfully recollect, we make a record by writing it down. Likewise, when the burden of accounting for reciprocity exceeds our ability to simply remember the details, we invent ledgers.

The earliest known records from ancient civilizations are clay tablets that seem to describe debt obligations. Mesopotamian cuneiform tablets describe banking records[37], and even earlier than that, a 20,000 year old Ishango Bone was found to have tally marks for correspondence counting[38]. It's hard to say whether money is older than writing or the reverse because our earliest examples of writing seem to be about debt.

Money is a Transferable Debt Obligation

Recording debts by writing them down is an ancient human behavior and it's still with us today. For example, you may have had the experience of writing an IOU to a friend. Your IOU is a tiny, one line ledger of a debt to be repaid.

Ledgers are excellent, but they have limits. Your friend may be able to transfer your IOU to another mutual friend, but a complete stranger who doesn't know you probably wouldn't accept it. This is where another ingenious technology—money—really shines.

From a certain point of view, money is a transferable debt obligation. It is a widely accepted, standardized, unitized, interchangeable IOU. With money, you don't need to consult or update a ledger to transfer a debt.

Whoever holds the money is the one who is owed, and a debt is discharged when the money changes hands[39]. Put differently, money (or, more specifically,

cash) is a one line ledger that omits the parties involved, specifying only the amount of the debt. This is
true whether we're talking about trading shell beads,
gold coins, cigarettes or paper bills.

Because it encodes a debt, people will accept a monetary good as payment even though its primary value is
only that someone else will accept it later in kind. This
monetary behavior is the technological extension of
our proclivity to initiate, record, distribute and protect
acts of reciprocal investment[40].

Engaging in reciprocal investment is vital to human
flourishing. The degree to which we can accomplish it
depends on the quality of the money that we use. We
need good money so that we can reliably store and
transfer value across time and distance—the longer
and the further the better.

Bitcoin is Global Fair Money

When it comes to being good money, fiat currency
doesn't fit the bill. While it's true that fiat currency is
widely accepted as a means of payment, it's also inherently unfair. By design, when new credit money is created from nothing, it transfers your purchasing power
to the State, the banks and the wealthy. Our human
proclivity to engage in reciprocal investment is cheated
by entrenched third parties who control the issuance of
the currency, and then direct it for special interests.

Bitcoin is different. Instead of being tied to a particular jurisdiction, Bitcoin is native to the Internet. It's worldwide. And rather than forever increasing in amount at no cost (which would steal your purchasing power like fiat does) the total future supply of Bitcoin is known and capped. Its issuance is predictable, decentralized, verifiable and open.

Bitcoin is global fair money. Let's see how it works.

CHAPTER 3
Down the Rabbit Hole

When Bitcoiners reflect on how they got into Bitcoin, they sometimes refer to it as their journey down the rabbit hole, a reference to Lewis Carroll's iconic book *Alice's Adventures in Wonderland*. Alice, chasing the white rabbit, fell into the rabbit hole and discovered Wonderland—an inverted world teeming with strange characters and vibrating with detail[41].

Learning about Bitcoin is like this. You start with a seemingly straightforward goal: to understand what appears to be a new technology. What is it? How does it work? The next thing you know, you're studying a dozen different fields from cryptography to macroeconomics to social psychology. You may even begin to question some of what you thought you knew on subjects like money and governance. Perhaps your own rabbit hole journey has already begun.

In this chapter, we'll take a tour of Wonderland and create a map of the territory. You'll learn how Bitcoin consists of three interdependent parts: one part social, one part technological and one part monetary. Each part operates by consensus. We'll enumerate some key subtopics of each part and we'll explore how they interrelate. Next we'll zoom out and survey the surrounding area—the places where Bitcoin's social, technological and monetary parts come into contact with the rest of the world.

The map that we develop here will help to guide us as we dig into specific subtopics, so let's get to it!

Defining Bitcoin

When people encounter Bitcoin for the first time, they often start with the question, "what is it?" This is a natural question, but it's also a challenging one to answer because Bitcoin really isn't like anything else. It's a whole new thing.

You can think of Bitcoin as having three parts: one social, one technological and one monetary. Declaratively, we can say that Bitcoin is three things: a programmable money, a computer network, and a social phenomenon.

These three parts form the center of our map. The following figure shows them in a circle to indicate the relationships between them.

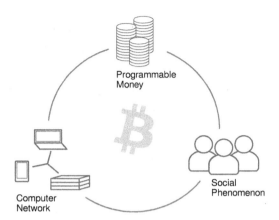

Bitcoin's three parts are mutually reinforcing and inseparable. Let's discuss each in turn, then pull them together. Because most folks hear about Bitcoin first as a monetary good (as in, the price of Bitcoin), we'll start there, and move on to the technological and social parts.

Bitcoin is Consensual Programmable Money

Bitcoin is a kind of digital money. When people talk about buying Bitcoin, or the current price of Bitcoin, this is what they mean.

Bitcoin is *consensual* in many senses of the word. Unlike fiat currencies, no one is forced to use or accept Bitcoin. The conditions of its use are controlled entirely by its users. These conditions can be written into the transactions themselves, making Bitcoin more than just digital—it is consensual, programmable money.

Amounts of Bitcoin are stored in a global, distributed ledger called the blockchain, which you can think of like a big spreadsheet of numbered accounts. When you have some Bitcoin, what you really have is the ability to transfer amounts of Bitcoin from some of these accounts to other numbered accounts. (Technically speaking, Bitcoin uses a transaction model, not an account model, a distinction we'll explore in Part II).

The total amount of Bitcoin that could ever exist is capped at just under ₿21 million. This might not sound like much, but each Bitcoin is divisible into smaller units, just like dollars or euros can be subdivided into cents. The smallest unit of Bitcoin is called a *sat* (short for *satoshi*) which is one one-hundred-millionth (1/100,000,000) of a Bitcoin. As a decimal, that's ₿0.00000001. In total, this means there will eventually be slightly fewer than 2.1 quadrillion (2,100,000,000,000,000) sats[42].

As of the year 2020, over ₿18 million has entered circulation, roughly 85% of the total supply. But due to Bitcoin's diminishing issuance schedule, the final sat won't enter circulation until approximately 2140[43].

Bitcoin is a Global Computer Network

Bitcoin is a peer-to-peer computer network that maintains the integrity of the blockchain.

This network is a mix of different kinds of *nodes*—computer programs that intercommunicate. Some nodes keep a full copy of all transactions that have gone into making the ledger. Other nodes only track changes to particular accounts of interest.

Still other nodes are engaged in the industrial activity known as mining—the process of securely adding blocks to the blockchain in accordance with the network consensus rules. This proof of work (PoW) is the key innovation that makes the Bitcoin network a permissionless system and protects it from centralization and censorship.

Bitcoin is a Social Phenomenon

Bitcoin is a social phenomenon made of many kinds of people. The rules of consensus that govern the Bitcoin computer network are established through a complex process involving different parties with sometimes conflicting interests.

In the earliest days, the social element of Bitcoin was entirely comprised of technologists—programmers and researchers working on the Bitcoin technology. Over time, more and different kinds of people have joined. These include miners who run increasingly large scale mining operations, merchants who accept Bitcoin as payment and entrepreneurs with Bitcoin-focused companies such as exchanges.

Putting this all together: Bitcoin is consensual, programmable money that is stored on the blockchain, secured by proof of work and governed by consensus. It is a complex adaptive system that consists of social, technological and monetary parts and all the connections and interactions between those parts.

It's no coincidence that all three of these meanings are present in the title of the Bitcoin white paper, *Bitcoin: A Peer-to-Peer Electronic Cash System*:

- *Peer-to-Peer* — The social aspect of Bitcoin has no formal hierarchy. All participants operate consensually as peers.

- *Electronic* — The computer network of Bitcoin enforces a purely digital protocol. Electricity is the bridge between the natural and digital worlds.

- *Cash System* — The value that flows through the network settles like cash. Sats are not credit instruments, but rather digital bearer assets.

It's crucial to understand that Bitcoin is all three of these interrelated parts. Without any of the three components—money, technology or people—the system could not exist in its present form, or perhaps at all.

Without the money aspect of Bitcoin, there wouldn't be as much incentive for people to work on and maintain the technology. Without the technology, Bitcoin would at best be a private currency subject to disruption by attacks. And without the social element, Bitcoin would just be a niche form of distributed database.

Now that we've established this three-part definition of Bitcoin, let's talk about how each part is governed by consensus.

Establishing Consensus

Bitcoin operates on consensus, and just as there are three parts to Bitcoin, there are three kinds of consensus: social, technological and monetary.

- *Social* — Social consensus is a semi-structured process by which people come to agree on the rules that govern the computer network.

- *Technological* — Technological consensus (or network consensus) is a rigorous, algorithmic process by which nodes in the Bitcoin network arrive at a consistent view of the ledger maintained by the blockchain.

- *Monetary* — Monetary consensus is the market process by which people establish what sats (amounts of Bitcoin) are worth in exchange for other things. This is also called price discovery.

All forms of consensus making are messy. Consider social consensus. Finding a set of rules that everyone can agree on can be very challenging. There are trade-offs to weigh and consider. Different people have different points of view, different values. Debates among Bitcoiners can be, at times, quite fierce.

The computer network of Bitcoin nodes also engages in messy consensus seeking, though it's perhaps less obvious because it happens at the protocol level. Each node in the network has its own limited view of the whole, from which it has to establish the state of the blockchain. Some nodes are misconfigured and relay bad data. Other nodes may be actively trying to subvert the network. The Bitcoin computer network has survived as long as it has not because it hasn't been attacked, but rather the opposite. It has been under attack virtually since day one.

Lastly, if you've been watching the Bitcoin price, you'll know that finding monetary consensus is a messy business. The volatility in the price of Bitcoin has been staggering compared to many other assets.

But none of this should be all that surprising. If you've ever tried to get a group of people to agree on something, you've probably found that coming to consensus is difficult any time that there isn't clear guidance to go on. And it gets more difficult the more people that are involved and the higher the stakes.

Over time, Bitcoin has attracted a larger and more varied crowd, and its price (while volatile) has generally increased. Both the number and diversity of folks have been rising along with the value at stake. We can expect that reaching social consensus on any proposed changes to Bitcoin is only going to get harder.

But there is no alternative because none of the three forms of Bitcoin consensus can be short-circuited by an authority figure. There's no leader who can unilaterally decide which rules the Bitcoin computer network will follow. There's no node in the Bitcoin network that can impose its view of the blockchain state on other nodes. And there's no bureaucrat who can set the price of Bitcoin against any other good or currency.

Bitcoin's three interconnected parts and consensus-based governance make it a new kind of system. Previous efforts to organize human affairs at scale relied on trusted intermediaries and formal hierarchy. Bitcoin replaces privilege with consensus.

Charting a Map of Bitcoin

Now let's continue our quest to map Wonderland. We'll start by listing some key subtopics of Bitcoin's social, technological and monetary parts. After that, we'll zoom out and chart the social, technological and monetary environments with which Bitcoin interacts.

Starting with Bitcoin's social part, we have HODLers ('hodl' is an intentional misspelling of 'hold'[44]), Researchers, Developers and Miners. It is the people of Bitcoin—the Bitcoiners—that ultimately give value to the Bitcoin project and so we'll discuss them right away in the next chapter.

Bitcoin's technological part includes Software, Hardware, Nodes and Protocols. In the chapters of Part II, we'll step through the process of getting set up with Bitcoin and receiving some for the first time. During this walkthrough, you'll be exposed to much of Bitcoin's technology stack.

In Bitcoin's monetary part, we find Value, Payments, Smart Contracts and Issuance. The union of Bitcoin's three parts gives rise to a monetary medium uniquely suited to being global, fair money. We'll discuss Bitcoin's monetary properties in Part III.

Zooming out, just as Bitcoin has social, technological and monetary parts, the environment that it inhabits can be thought of in the same terms. Let's go through each.

Bitcoin's Social Environment

Bitcoin's social environment includes industry players like Merchants, Entrepreneurs and Traders. It also includes governmental bodies: Lawmakers, Regulators and Law Enforcement. The Bankers who operate the traditional banking sector appear here, as does the mainstream media.

Of course, this is not an exhaustive list of everyone in the world outside of Bitcoin, and these aren't always cleanly separable groups. For example, an entrepreneur who starts a Bitcoin payment processing company might also be a developer who contributes code to Bitcoin. The membrane between Bitcoin and its environment is a porous one.

Bitcoin's Technological Environment

In Bitcoin's technological environment you'll find Computing, Networking, and Algorithms. Manufacturing plays a role in who mines Bitcoin and where and how.

Two bridge technologies worth noting are Energy and Exchanges. Energy—in the form of electricity—is the bridge between the natural and digital worlds. Electricity powers our modern lives, and it also enables the calculations done by our computers.

Exchanges bridge the Bitcoin value network and the traditional banking system. Using exchanges, people can buy Bitcoin using their local currency.

Altcoins—short for alternative coins—are other cryptocurrency networks and tokens. They are frequently but not always based on Bitcoin, sometimes differing only in tiny details, and other times using a different technology stack. Altcoins are occasionally sources of innovation, trying out more experimental ideas before they're adopted into consensus Bitcoin.

Bitcoin's Monetary Environment

Bitcoin's monetary environment includes things like Currencies, Commodities, Securities and their Derivatives. Competing stores of value like Real Estate and Equities appear here, as well as Debt and Price. The Price of Bitcoin is what grabs headlines. Price is the subject of endless speculation from both the mainstream media and social media alike.

A ratio between Bitcoin's units and some other currency, the price of Bitcoin is a reflection of the overall market sentiment toward the project, factoring in all of the knowledge—special and public alike—of all market participants. It is set by everyone and by no one in particular.

Putting all these topics together yields the following map:

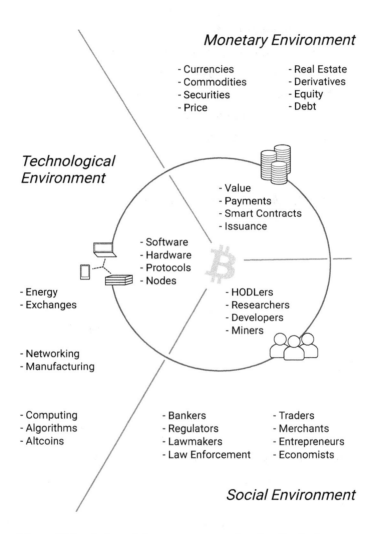

Map of Bitcoin's social, monetary and technological parts,
and the environments in which they operate.

The question at the heart of this book is "how can a purely digital money that's not backed by anything have any value to people at all?" To answer this question, we'll stick mostly to topics inside the circle—the Bitcoin consensus. Later books in this series will explore the interactions between Bitcoin and its environment.

Now that we've sketched out a map of the Bitcoin territory, let's visit the people that inhabit it: Bitcoiners.

CHAPTER 4

Meeting the People of Bitcoin

When critics complain that Bitcoin isn't backed by anything, what they mean is that unlike sovereign currency which is backed by an issuing government, or gold which is backed by industrial uses, Bitcoin has little non-monetary use. And it's true. Bitcoin's only purpose is to provide an incorruptible, uncensorable, decentralized, permissionless ledger.

But despite the critics' claims, Bitcoin is backed by Bitcoiners[45]. In this chapter, we'll discuss some of the people of Bitcoin—the social phenomenon that imbues the monetary units and computer network with purpose. You'll discover the subtle ways in which they depend on each other and how this makes Bitcoin robust. Specifically, you'll learn about the HODLers, researchers, developers and miners that make up Bitcoin. We'll also discuss traders and merchants and their roles.

It is the people of Bitcoin that ultimately give Bitcoin its value. Let's start by discussing the HODLers.

HODLers

Unlike traders, who actively buy and sell Bitcoin, some people *HODL*—an intentional misspelling of the word "HOLD", which has become a rallying cry[46]. HODLers use Bitcoin as a store of value.

Generally speaking, HODLers behave as though they accept the central premise of this book series, that Bitcoin will become the way we measure all intersubjective value. Rather than trying to sell when the price of Bitcoin has reached a recent high point in fiat currency terms, HODLers expect that what you can buy with a Bitcoin will vastly exceed the current price over the long-term.

From the perspective of a HODLer, holding a quantity of Bitcoin is like staking out territory. Each sat represents a fixed proportion of all there can ever be. Since money exists to serve as a transferrable debt obligation, and the supply of sats is capped, each sat is a claim of fixed proportion on the future productive output of humanity in perpetuity.

HODLers' desire to store wealth in Bitcoin provides the non-zero lower bound on Bitcoin value and thus price[47]. As long as there are HODLers HODLing, Bitcoin will be worth something.

In the short-term, HODLers rely on traders who provide market liquidity and price discovery (monetary consensus). And in the long-term, HODLers need merchants who will accept Bitcoin as payment for goods and services.

HODLers also rely on the fundamental value of the Bitcoin network as a secure, distributed ledger that records everyone's Bitcoin balances. To protect this resource, HODLers often run their own fully validating nodes, making them fully sovereign participants in Bitcoin's consensus.

Anyone, anywhere can volunteer to run a validating Bitcoin node and thereby ensure that new transactions follow the rules of the network. But a special kind of network participant, called a miner, works to create the ledger that's secured and validated by everyone.

Let's talk about miners and the work they do, next.

Miners

Miners are folks who run specialized, high-powered computers that compete with each other to add new records to Bitcoin's ledger. The work done by miners to secure the ledger in the blockchain is the key technological innovation that makes Bitcoin incorruptible, fair money.

We'll discuss mining and miners throughout this book series, but for now you should know that the Bitcoin computer network automatically adjusts to changes in the level of competition. When more miners join to compete for blocks, the difficulty automatically increases to make sure that the average time between blocks stays right around ten minutes.

Because the level of competition between miners generally keeps increasing, running mining hardware takes a lot of electricity. But as compensation for mining a block, the miner receive a *block reward* of Bitcoin.

At the time of this writing, the reward per block mined is ₿6.25 (625 million sats). This amount gets cut in half every four years (every 210,000 blocks to be precise), with the next halving to occur around May, 2024, when the block reward will drop to ₿3.125 (312.5 million sats). The block reward is how new sats enter circulation. There is no other way to increase the circulating supply of Bitcoin, which means that as mining becomes more attractive, new miners serve to increase competition and further secure the network.

Because mining has become so difficult, and new blocks are consistently scarce (just one every 10 minutes), miners often team up to form *mining pools*. This is a lot like a lottery pool, where people combine their resources and agree to share the prize if they happen to win. Some mining pools are free to join by anyone and others are private enterprises. It's relatively easy for a miner to switch pools, so the relative strengths of the pools fluctuate.

Since they almost always pay their electricity bills in local currency, miners need exchanges through which to sell their Bitcoin to traders and HODLers. They also rely on developers who write and maintain the Bitcoin software that they run.

Developers and Researchers

Anyone who writes software to support Bitcoin is a developer. This could be software for a wallet, for a fully validating node or for specialized mining software. Some developers write software to support exchanges or for payment processors used by merchants. Some are paid employees of companies working full time on Bitcoin and related technologies. Many others are volunteers, contributing in their off-hours.

Researchers study the various social, technical and monetary aspects of Bitcoin and produce artifacts of their findings such as articles and white papers. Sometimes researchers discover bugs or threats to Bitcoin. Other times they propose changes which could improve features of Bitcoin such as security, privacy or efficiency.

The most popular fully validating Bitcoin node software, Bitcoin Core, is staffed by some of the most prolific and influential developers, who claim the title "Bitcoin Core Developer". Don't be confused. There is no official Bitcoin organization. The name Bitcoin Core is clever marketing, as is the title Bitcoin Core Developer.

The first developer of Bitcoin was an anonymous person—or possibly a group of people—using the pseudonym Satoshi Nakamoto. On October 31, 2008, Satoshi published a white paper titled *Bitcoin: A Peer-to-Peer Electronic Cash System* and then released the first version of the Bitcoin code (v0.1.0) on January 9, 2009. This software would become the basis of the Bitcoin Core code.

Satoshi was last active in Bitcoin in December, 2010, and has disappeared entirely save for one comment in 2014 when a Japanese gentleman named Dorian Nakamoto was mistakenly misidentified as Satoshi. This final message stated simply "I am not Dorian Nakamoto"[48], and nothing more has been heard from Satoshi since.

Some developers are in Bitcoin for the long haul, expecting it to become the measure of all intersubjective value. Others are into Bitcoin because it's the current hot thing, especially blockchain technology which has become something of a buzzword.

No matter what their long-term vision, developers want to see their software used, and to good effect. To that end, developers rely on everyone in the network to imbue their work with purpose. Without users, there's no point in putting forth the effort.

Let's talk about some of those users next: traders.

Traders

A trader is someone who buys and sells Bitcoin and other assets with the hope of profiting from fluctuations in prices over time. Traders can have a big impact on the day-to-day price of Bitcoin, but this is not their most important role.

Traders perform two important functions for the long-term viability of Bitcoin. They provide market liquidity, and their speculative behavior is a fundamental use case for the network. Let's talk about each of these functions, starting with liquidity.

Providing Market Liquidity

Liquidity is a financial term which relates to how easy it is to buy or sell something without affecting its price. Assets that are liquid can be bought or sold quickly without making the price change too much. Illiquid assets, by contrast, are more difficult to exchange.

When traders think the price of Bitcoin will go up, they buy, and when they think it'll go down they sell. Each trader brings a particular viewpoint to the market.

The more diverse the pool of traders, the less variable the price becomes, because they crowd around the market price and fill in gaps in the order book. A precise explanation of how an order book works is outside the scope of this chapter, but suffice it to say that more traders, acting independently, tend to lead toward monetary consensus.

However, there is an important caveat: people do not always act independently and rationally. The old adage of investing is "buy low, sell high," but this is easier said than done. Newcomers tend to arrive to Bitcoin in waves, and inexperienced traders are subject to especially impulsive, emotion-driven behavior.

Emotion-driven traders unfortunately often buy on the upswing and then panic sell when the price drops, thinking they need to protect their principal while they can. This can lead to a certain amount of herd mentality, causing cycles of positive and negative sentiment (so-called bull and bear markets).

Now, let's discuss the other crucial function that traders provide, the gambling use case.

Gambling on Bitcoin

By engaging in speculative buying and selling, traders supply a reason for Bitcoin to continue to exist, if only so they can gamble on its exchange rate. Granted, traders have other opportunities, but speculative trading on Bitcoin is a self-regulating activity, backstopped by HODLers.

Increased diversity of traders leads to a more stable price. But the inverse is also true. The fewer people there are trading Bitcoin, the more volatile its price due to lower liquidity. Increased volatility makes it a more attractive vehicle for short-term speculation (gambling) which invites traders back in.

The desire to gamble on the price fluctuations of Bitcoin provides a certain kind of use-case. As long as there are even a tiny number of speculators, Bitcoin will have a non-zero price and therefore afford continued trading.

Lastly, let's talk about merchants who accept Bitcoin and the customers who use it to make purchases.

Merchants

Customers who spend Bitcoin to buy goods and services, and the merchants who accept it, form the last group of people we'll discuss. These are the adventurous and rare early adopters—pioneers of the use case of regular commerce.

We're still in the very early stages of Bitcoin's adoption as a means of payment for regular, everyday purchases. To a certain degree, it's a chicken-and-egg problem. Customers who want to pay with Bitcoin need merchants to accept it, and merchants are reluctant to put forth the effort unless there is customer demand.

Widespread adoption faces a number of additional hurdles, some technical, some social, and some regulatory. For just one example, recall that new blocks are added to the blockchain about once every 10 minutes. When a transaction is mined into a block, this counts as one *confirmation*. It's typical for a recipient to want six confirmations (five more blocks) to consider a transaction settled.

Waiting 10, 20 or 60 minutes to complete a transaction is too long for small, everyday purchases. For this reason, Bitcoin critics are quick to say you wouldn't use Bitcoin to buy a cup of coffee. (Emerging solutions like the Lightning Network are improving the situation, but we'll save that discussion for later.)

Nevertheless, some early adopters of Bitcoin who have seen its value rise over time are looking to spend. And merchants willing to cater to them can charge a premium. As Bitcoin increasingly becomes the metric of all intersubjective value, pressure from long-time holders who want to spend will encourage merchant adoption[49].

Now that we've discussed the types of people that make up the Bitcoin ecosystem, let's investigate the relationships between the groups and what it means for Bitcoin.

Intergroup Dynamics

In this chapter, we discussed HODLers, miners, researchers, developers as well as traders and merchants who use Bitcoin. Each has a role to play in the short, medium and long term, and, to a greater or lesser degree, each group depends on the others. At the same time, the groups have interdependent and occasionally conflicting goals that lead to a strong status quo bias for all participants.

Traders, HODLers and merchants provide important use cases for the Bitcoin network. Some use it to effect payments, others as a store of value, or just to gamble on price volatility. These users rely on the stability of the underlying network in order to effect transfers, and are naturally averse to changes which would put that stability in jeopardy.

HODLers and merchants are incented to run their own fully validating Bitcoin nodes. For HODLers, this is a way to ensure beyond doubt that the network continues to abide by the rules they've agreed to, such as the strictly limited lifetime supply of ₿21 million. For merchants, running a full node allows them to independently verify when they've received payment from a customer, without relying on a third party.

Miners are compensated in Bitcoin for adding new blocks of transactions to the blockchain. If a miner attempts to mine a block with bad transactions, these blocks will be rejected by the fully validating nodes, rendering the miner's investment of hardware and electricity worthless. Likewise, in order to sell the Bitcoin they are awarded for mining, miners are incented to uphold the network's integrity. It's more profitable to follow the consensus rules than to try to break them.

The developers who write the software are incentivized to stay within the consensus rules too. A developer attempting to introduce a change to the parameters of the Bitcoin network faces the daunting challenge of convincing node operators to adopt the change by installing their version of the software. While it's easy to make a change to the code—like editing a local copy of an online file—if it breaks the consensus rules it's incredibly difficult to muster enough support from the other participants to make it a lasting change.

A successful change to the Bitcoin network's consensus rules requires virtually all node operators to agree. Bitcoin's extremely high consensus requirement ensures that only the best ideas, those consented to unanimously, become adopted.

Critics sometimes say that Bitcoin isn't backed by anything, but this is not true. This ecosystem of co-dependent parties—the people of Bitcoin—is ultimately what gives Bitcoin its value.

Now that we've established that the value of Bitcoin originates from the people of Bitcoin, let's continue to

Part II where we'll explore the question of how the Bitcoin technology works.

PART II

How does Bitcoin work (for you)?

CHAPTER 5

Setting Up Your First Wallet

To understand how Bitcoin—the programmable, consensual money—can have any value to anyone at all, you kind of have to know how it works. At least, you need to know how it works for you. In this chapter, you'll learn some of the technical side of Bitcoin as we follow the process of setting up a wallet step by step.

This journey will expose you to many of the technical aspects of Bitcoin. We won't go into every conceivable detail—there's too much for that—but this will provide a ground level view of the relevant components. This will naturally lead into the following chapter where you'll learn how to receive sats into your freshly created wallet.

A Word of Warning

Working with Bitcoin, at the time of this writing, is a bit like working with the Internet in the 1990's in the sense that the user experience has not yet caught up with the technological possibilities.

It took years for concepts like the World-Wide Web (www) and email to get refined, reimagined and even-

tually folded into the fabric of everyday existence[50].
Bitcoin isn't there yet, and so the experience is still
fairly technical (though it's getting smoother all the
time).

As a result, this is probably going to seem harder
than it really is. Later entrants to the Bitcoin ecosystem
won't have to learn these things like you are doing because it'll be a natural part of everyday life. Some of the
concepts will be second nature (like we think of web
pages and mobile apps today) and many of the details
will be woven into the apps and devices people have at
hand.

It's also the case that most of those future users just
won't care how Bitcoin works. And why should they?
The world is filled with invisible technology that's be-
wilderingly complex to the lay person and which only
trained experts know how to command. Consider a
typical microwave oven. You don't need to understand
the physics of dielectric heating to operate it, just
which buttons to press.

But that's also partly what makes Bitcoin an opportunity. If it was easy, everyone would be doing it. And
they will, just not yet.

And so here we are, about to inspect the journey of a
Bitcoin transaction in much the same way that a previous generation might study the journey of receiving
their first email in 1994. Fortunately, the two proce-
dures are not all that different. The following table of-

fers a comparison of the nine steps to receiving your first email and receiving your first Bitcoin. Steps marked with an asterisk (*) you only do the first time.

	Email	Bitcoin
1	Find a service provider.*	Download a wallet.*
2	Pick a good password.*	Generate a random seed.*
3	Record password in a safe place.*	Write down the seed's mnemonic code.*
4	Choose an available email address.*	Generate a Bitcoin address.
5	Tell the sender your email address.	Tell the sender your Bitcoin address.
6	Sender composes a message.	Sender creates a transaction.
7	Sender sends message to server.	Sender broadcasts transaction to network.
8	Email server relays message.	Bitcoin miner adds transaction to blockchain.
9	Service provider displays message.	Wallet shows funds received.

It's easy to forget how many steps are involved in something as mundane as receiving an email! As you scan the steps in the left-hand column of this table, take note of how many of these concepts would have been new to someone without prior email experience.

Notice that the first three steps of receiving your Bitcoin only happen the first time. Those are the steps we'll walk through in the remainder of this chapter. Next chapter is devoted to the rest of the steps—the ones that happen each time you receive Bitcoin.

For now, let's start at the beginning and talk about getting a wallet.

Download a Wallet

Email equivalent: Find a service provider.

The first step to receiving any amount of Bitcoin is acquiring a wallet. Your wallet is the piece of software that lets you read and write to Bitcoin's global distributed ledger, which is secured by the blockchain. There are wallet apps that run on smartphones and applications that run on general purpose computers.

There are lots of software wallets to choose from, and you should take care when deciding among them.

Consider whether the software is Open Source. If it is, then you or someone else can audit its code. If the software is closed source, then you're placing a significantly higher level of trust in the developers of that software.

All software has the potential of having bugs—unforeseen mistakes in the code. At least with open source software, well intentioned outside developers can review the code and point out trouble spots to the creators. With closed source software, often it is only bad actors that find (and exploit) vulnerabilities.

My advice: Do your own research and use an open source wallet.

Many wallet apps, especially on mobile devices, support protection via a PIN code. Setting up a PIN is a good security practice to help prevent anyone from accessing your funds.

Generate a Random Seed

Email equivalent: Pick a good password.

The most crucial job of your wallet is safeguarding your private keys. These cryptographic keys are very large (256 bit) numbers. Your private keys are the only things that give you control over your Bitcoin balances. If anyone else ever has access to your keys, you should consider your Bitcoin balance to be compromised, and you should seek to transfer it to a new wallet based on secure keys as soon as you can.

Your private keys are generated from a large random number called a *seed*. Although the seed itself is just a number, many wallets implement an encoding scheme that represents it as a sequence of 12 to 24 words called a *mnemonic code* or *seed phrase*. Each word in the phrase corresponds to an index into a dictionary of 2048 possible words[51]. Thus each word represents 11 bits of information because it takes 11 bits to represent any number from 0 to 2047.

Write Down the Mnemonic Code

Email equivalent: Record password in a safe place.

If there's one thing you take away from this setup process, it should be this: unlike your email password, your private keys cannot be recovered if lost. If you lose your keys, you lose all of your Bitcoin.

There is no one to go to if you lose your private keys. There is no help line or service department. You must keep these in a safe place.

Key management is the most difficult problem in cryptography[52], so full treatment of how to safeguard your keys is outside the scope of this book. But here are a few tips:

- Order matters! When you write down your seed phrase, it's good practice to use lined paper and include the number of each word so there can be no mistake.

- Confirm your seed words. Many wallets will prompt you to enter a word or two from your seed phrase to confirm that you've written them down correctly.

- Do not save the seed to a file. If you were to store your seed phrase in a text file (like a document), then an attacker with access to your computer could steal all your Bitcoin.

- Do not take a screenshot or photo. Even if the phrase words are pixels of an image instead of raw text, an attacker could still get them and steal all of your Bitcoin.

- Keep them secret. If anyone ever learns your seed phrase, they can steal all of your Bitcoin.

- Keep them safe. Protect your hand-written seed words from natural disasters like pests, water damage and fire.

Most importantly, no matter what,

DO NOT SAVE YOUR SEED TO A FILE

In your regular life as a computer user, it's common practice to save important information to files for safe keeping. This is inappropriate and dangerous for your

Bitcoin private keys. No matter how clean you think your computer is, the possibility remains that a latent virus or a determined attacker could find that file and steal all of your Bitcoin at any future time.

To use an analogy, you can imagine guarding your private keys like keeping surgery tools sterile. The patient on the operating table is your Bitcoin, locked in the blockchain. Your wallet is the surgeon, using the tools (private keys) to make small changes safely.

Your computer is the hospital. You try to keep it clean, and it looks pretty good, but who knows what viruses and maladies are festering in the rooms next door. Saving your seed to a file is like taking those sterile surgical instruments and leaving them on a coffee table in the lobby. Who knows what might infect them there? What could a random visitor do with them?

Bitcoin wallets take great care to guard your private keys by keeping them encrypted. The rest of your computer system may not take such precautions. If your seed ever appears as text in your computer, you should consider that seed compromised and seek to set up a new seed.

Now that you have your wallet installed, you've generated a private key and you've written down the seed phrase, the one-time setup steps are complete and you're ready to receive some Bitcoin. Continue to the next chapter to see how.

CHAPTER 6

Receiving Your First Bitcoin

Last chapter, we walked through the three step process of setting up a Bitcoin wallet for the first time. Those steps you only need to do once. Here we continue that journey, walking through the six steps to receiving Bitcoin into your wallet. The steps are:

1. Generate a Bitcoin address.
2. Tell the sender your Bitcoin address.
3. Sender creates a transaction.
4. Sender broadcasts the transaction.
5. Miner adds transaction to the blockchain.
6. Wallet shows funds received.

Don't worry if this looks complicated, the steps become second nature once you've done them a few times. Let's go through them one by one. Just like last chapter, we'll equate each with the equivalent step one would perform to receive an email.

Generate a Bitcoin Address

Email equivalent: Choose an available email address.

In the email example, your password and your address are separate things. When you log in, your email service provider makes sure that your address and password match up, but you can change your password (and sometimes your email address) independently of the other.

Not so in Bitcoin. Because Bitcoin is trust minimizing, there is no service provider who keeps track of the relationship between your private keys and your public addresses.

Instead, when you want to receive some Bitcoin, your wallet will generate a public address for you based on your private key. Each time you go to receive Bitcoin, the best practice is to generate a new address to give to the sender.

Technically speaking, it's possible to reuse an address once it has been generated. After all, your public addresses are derived from your private keys. A used address would still work for receiving funds if you forwarded it to someone else for payment. However, to enhance your privacy, the standard best practice is to only use each public address once. The reason for this will become clear in a bit when we talk about how transactions are recorded on the global public ledger.

Tell the Sender Your Bitcoin Address

Email equivalent: Tell the sender your email address.

To receive an email, the sender needs to know your email address. Likewise, to receive any Bitcoin, the sender needs to know your Bitcoin address. A Bitcoin address is a long string of random looking characters. There are several kinds of addresses and different ways of encoding them. For an example, here's a donation address for this book:

```
34yhFok9b3RdLGbPQpP58D3mp5W8hsU4pi
```

To provide your Bitcoin address to the sender, you can use any available medium that's capable of sending short amounts of text. If you use the bitcoin: protocol prefix, you can also include a requested amount as a URI. For example, here's the donation address for this book again, encoded as a bitcoin: URI, and including the suggested donation amount of ₿0.001:

```
bitcoin:34yhFok9b3RdLGbPQpP58D3mp5W8hsU4pi?amoun
t=0.00100000
```

If your device has a wallet installed and it has registered the bitcoin: protocol, then following that link would open your wallet app. Any good wallet will ask you to triple-check the details before sending, and if you've set up a PIN code, it should require that as well.

For in-person transactions, many wallets support encoding and scanning addresses as QR codes, which are like two-dimensional bar codes. Here's a QR code for the same URI we discussed earlier that includes this book's donation address and suggested donation amount:

If you're reading this on physical paper, or on a different device than where your wallet is installed, you could use your wallet's scan feature to read this QR code. The scan feature uses the device's camera, so you may have to enable that access separately depending on your device's security settings. Once your wallet has scanned the QR code, it will give you the option to confirm or adjust the amount before sending. When a Bitcoin URI contains an amount requested, this is only a suggestion.

Irrespective of how you supply your Bitcoin address to the sender, it's crucial that they check to make sure it is correct. Security researchers have found malware

that monitors for Bitcoin addresses in victims' clip-
boards and replaces them with the attackers' addresses[53]. So it's always good practice to reconfirm at
least the first few and last few characters of the address
before hitting 'send'.

Sender Generates a Transaction

Email equivalent: Sender composes a message.

Once the sender has your Bitcoin address, they can
create a transaction that assigns some of their Bitcoin
value to you. You can think of a transaction kind of like
a traditional bank check, in that it contains much of the
same information. It has an identifier, from/to fields,
an amount to send, and a signature.

Sender Broadcasts the Transaction to the Network

Email equivalent: Sender sends message to server.

After the sender has finished creating the transaction, their wallet broadcasts it to the Bitcoin network. Each node in the network checks the transaction for correctness and then passes it along to other nodes to which that node is connected (peer-to-peer). If the transaction was invalid for any reason, the first node that received it would reject it (and also break off communications with the sender for having forwarded the bad transaction). This way, only valid transactions propagate through the network.

As nodes receive the transaction, they put it in their list of pending transactions called the *mempool*. This is a local holding area where transactions wait to be confirmed into a block. Since it takes time for transactions to propagate to all the nodes in the network, there will be minor discrepancies between nodes' mempools with regards to which transactions they contain. Pretty quickly though, the transaction will have made it to most of the nodes in the network.

Bitcoin Miner Adds the Transaction to the Blockchain

Email equivalent: Email server relays message.

Even though the transaction has been validated and propagated, it's too early to declare that your funds have been received. Think of the old saying "the check's in the mail." You can verify that the transaction has been sent by probing your node's mempool, but until the transaction is settled on the blockchain, the prudent thing to do is to wait.

Bitcoin miners operate nodes in the network that, in addition to validating and propagating transactions, also mine new blocks of transactions. Mining is essentially the process of trying to guess a very large random number that meets particular cryptographic criteria. Without going into the details too much, this requires performing a small amount of computation to make a guess at a random number and then check if it works. The vast majority of such guesses will be be wrong, and so very many guesses are made before a miner guesses a valid number for the block.

Bitcoin mining is a competitive industry that requires no special permissions to join or leave. Just as you are free to use Bitcoin or not, miners come and go as they please.

Eventually, a miner will mine a block that includes your transaction. That block propagates throughout the network just like the transaction did earlier. Nodes on the network validate every aspect of the block and all the transactions that it contains, then forward the block to other nodes to which they're connected. At that point, miners begin working on the next block of transactions, continuing the blockchain.

When your transaction has been mined into a block, this counts as one confirmation. Some time later, a miner (it could be the same one, or it could be a different one) will find another block on top of the block that includes your transaction. Now your transaction has two confirmations, and so on.

There's no one-size-fits-all rule to describe how many confirmations you need to consider a transaction finally settled. Picking a threshold has to do with your own risk tolerance, which should be informed by the amount of value being transferred. For very small amounts, low numbers of confirmations are probably fine. As the amount of Bitcoin you receive goes up, you'll want more and more confirmations. Six confirmations is a common baseline number used by many people in the community for medium sized transfers.

Wallet Shows Funds Received

Email equivalent: Service provider displays message.

As soon as your incoming transaction hit the mempool, your wallet should have shown something about it. Many wallets would show such a transaction as 'pending' or 'unconfirmed'.

A good wallet will tell you when the transaction has been mined into a block by changing the display in some way. It might have a percentage completion bar, or show the number of confirmations directly.

Once the transaction has reached some threshold number of confirmations (usually six) the wallet should show the transaction as being completed. The funds are now ready to spend.

Technically speaking, the Bitcoin protocol allows transactions to spend amounts of Bitcoin as soon as they hit the mempool. So why should you wait for six confirmations?

Spending unconfirmed Bitcoin is dangerous. It's roughly the same as floating a check against a bank account that you expect to have money in it by the time the check eventually clears. Transactions that remain unconfirmed for too long can be dropped from the mempool, which makes other transactions that depend on them invalid.

It would be a bad user experience to go and spend your unconfirmed Bitcoin and only later find out that your transaction got rolled back because the parent never cleared. For this reason, many wallets will avoid or outright prohibit spending unconfirmed Bitcoin, if only to avoid angry customer feedback.

In any case, once the transaction has been confirmed on the blockchain, the Bitcoin value is yours and you're now able to spend it. Someone who wants to receive Bitcoin from you generates an address and provides it to you. Then you create and broadcast a transaction. Eventually that transaction is confirmed in the blockchain and then they can do with it as they please.

This probably still seems complicated, and that's OK. Just like with email, it becomes second nature after a few experiences. The best way to grok it is to give it a try.

Between this chapter and the previous, you've learned a bit about how Bitcoin works for you. We walked through the steps necessary to receive your first Bitcoin which resemble the steps to receiving your first email. You saw how your wallet is responsible for tracking Bitcoin amounts that you control and for safe-guarding your private keys.

To close out this Part of the book, in the next chapter we'll discuss the different kinds of wallets and their relative pros and cons. Let's get to it!

CHAPTER 7

Securing Your Bitcoin

The best way to learn how Bitcoin works for you is to try it out yourself. It's one thing to read about a technology, and quite another to experience it first hand. So if at all possible, I recommend that you install a wallet to get started with Bitcoin. In this chapter we'll talk about the kinds of wallets available for you to try.

As we've discussed, a Bitcoin wallet is a program that uses your private key to sign transactions. There are several different kinds of wallets, and which one to use depends on how you want to use it.

When we talk about different kinds of wallets, one important characteristic to consider is how *hot* or *cold* it is. The hotter a wallet is, the easier it is to spend funds out of it, and the colder it is, the harder it is to spend money out. It's usually fairly easy to get sats into a wallet, irrespective of how hot or cold it is for spending.

There's no practical limit to the number of wallets you can have, so it's common for Bitcoin users to have several wallets which serve different purposes. This is directly analogous to fiat currency. You might carry a little physical cash on your person for small transactions, and use a debit card tied to your bank account to secure and transfer larger amounts of money. The amount of value at stake should have an impact on how you choose to secure it.

Here's the spectrum of wallets from hottest to coldest: Online (Custodial), Software, Hardware, Paper. Let's dive into each of these kinds of wallets in turn.

Online Wallets

Online wallets are provided by third party companies. They can be standalone web applications or they can be integrated into online Bitcoin exchanges. The distinguishing feature of online wallets is that they're *custodial*. Rather than you managing your own private keys, with a custodial wallet, you're entrusting that duty to a service provider.

If you purchase Bitcoin on an exchange, the exchange will keep track of your Bitcoin balance. They can show you the amount of Bitcoin you've purchased as part of your account. With this kind of service, any transactions are handled by the service provider from their wallet using their private keys.

As a practicality, your online wallet with an exchange probably doesn't have a specific set of private keys just for you. Instead, your Bitcoins are co-mingled and stored along with everyone else's, and the nominal amount in your account is kept in a separate database controlled by the exchange.

Since you don't hold the private keys, the exchange is the custodian of your Bitcoin. This introduces you to *counter-party risk*. This is the risk that the exchange could lose your Bitcoin through negligence, fraud or by being hacked.

This is what happened to Mt. Gox—millions of holders' funds were lost when that exchange became insolvent.

My advice: only use online wallets for briefly exchanging between Bitcoin and fiat currency. As Andreas Antonopoulos says, "Your keys, your coins. Not your keys, not your coins."[54]

Software Wallets

Software wallets are programs that run on general purpose computing machines like a laptops, desktops, tablets, and phones. There are lots of software wallets to choose from, and you should take care when deciding among them.

Consider whether the software is Open Source. If it is, then you or someone else can audit the code. If the software is closed source, then you're placing a significantly higher level of trust in the developers of that software.

All software has the potential of having bugs—unforeseen mistakes in the code. At least with Open Source software, well intentioned outside developers can review the code and point out trouble spots to the software's maintainers. With closed source software, it's more likely to be bad actors (internal or external) who find and exploit vulnerabilities.

My advice: Use Open Source wallets.

When choosing a software wallet, make sure that it protects your private key, preferably by encrypting it. If the wallet stores the key on your device without encryption, there's a risk that malicious code running on your machine could read the key, and steal your Bitcoin with it.

My advice: Encrypt your private keys.

And just as a reminder: to protect yourself from loss or theft of the device that has the private key, you must make a handwritten copy of the seed's mnemonic code. This means that you can recover funds if you need to.

Hardware Wallets

A hardware wallet is a physical device capable of signing transactions and responsible for safeguarding your private keys. With a hardware wallet, your private keys never leave the device. It has its own tiny screen, which is used to show you information about each transaction you ask it to sign.

There are several reputable manufacturers of hardware wallets. It's important to do your own research when choosing one.

For maximum security, some hardware wallets will only show you the seed phrase once, when it is initialized. After that, you must securely store the seed phrase elsewhere. There's no way to get the device to read it back to you again. This prevents attackers from being able to extract your seed phrase and steal your Bitcoin, but it also means you must store the hand written seed phrase securely.

This arrangement may seem concerning. What if you lose the seed phrase that you've written down on paper? With no way to recover the seed phrase, the only thing to do is transfer all of the funds into a new address based on a new seed.

Simple key loss is one of the greatest risks when holding Bitcoin, so it's vital that you protect your seed phrase. This brings us to paper wallets, the coldest form of storage.

Paper Wallets

A paper wallet is one in which the private keys' seed exists only written on physical paper, and is not resident on any silicon (hardware or software). For example, after writing down the seed phrase and generating one or more addresses, you could wipe the device, and now the only record is the paper.

To take it another step further, you could memorize the word sequence, such that the only record is in your memory. This is called a *brain wallet*. The problem, of course, is that if you forget any part of the sequence, then the Bitcoin secured by that key is irrecoverable. People often overestimate their own ability to memorize material, so I cannot advise this strategy. Keep your seed on paper.

Generating a paper wallet securely represents a significant challenge. You can't print the private key from a software wallet using your desktop printer, because that printer itself could be compromised. You can't take a picture of it with your phone's camera, because the photo could be leaked and a malicious screen-reading program could scrape it.

For the ultimate step-by-step guide to generating secure private key seeds for cold storage, some Bitcoiners use the Glacier Protocol[55]. This 90+ page document describes a procedure for creating a secure offline wallet using off-the-shelf hardware. It requires using multiple sets of computers and USB keys from different manufacturers. For some of the computers, the Glacier Protocol requires that they have their network cards physically removed, and the devices can never be put online or connected to any unclean hardware. For extremely large amounts of Bitcoin, operational security of this kind may be warranted.

For a typical Bitcoiner, generating a seed mnemonic using a hardware wallet, transferring that to physical paper and then wiping the hardware device is probably good enough to create a long term cold storage wallet. If you do this, make sure you test the seed phrase by re-entering it into a wiped hardware wallet. This will confirm that in the future you'll be able to retrieve the funds.

Once you have your paper wallet, securing the paper is your highest priority. Traditional security mechanisms such as safes, private vaults and bank safety deposit boxes can be used.

No matter which option you choose for securing your Bitcoin, the effort you spend should be proportional to the value that it represents to you. As the value to you increases, make sure to revisit your security practices and make sure they're up to the job.

Multi-signature Wallets

Lastly, let's talk about multi-signature (multisig) wallets. A multisig wallet is one which requires signatures from more than one private key in order to spend.

For example, you could have a wallet for which there are five keys, any three of which are needed in order to spend any funds. This would be called a 3-of-5 multisig wallet. Typically wallets are described as M-of-N, where you need M keys out of N total keys to sign.

When securing your Bitcoin, there are two categories of risk to consider: risk of loss and risk of theft.

Loss is when you lose the keys by accident, and theft is when the keys are stolen by an attacker. Using a multisig wallet helps protect you from both kinds of risk. If you're using an M-of-N multisig wallet and you lose some of the keys, as long as there are still at least M keys left, you can recover your funds and move them to a new M-of-N wallet. Likewise, if an attacker manages to gain control of some of the keys, as long as they have fewer than M, they can't get your funds.

There are a growing number of service providers who offer to keep one key out of your multisig setup for safekeeping. For example, you could have a 2-of-3 multisig wallet where you keep one key on your device, the service provider keeps a second one, and the third exists only as a paper wallet backup. When you use the app to spend, your app signs with its key and you log into the service provider to get a second signature.

If your wallet app dies or its key is compromised, you can recover using the paper wallet and the provider. If the provider is compromised, you can recover using your app and the paper wallet. And if the paper wallet is destroyed, you can recover using your app and the provider.

Like other security decisions, there are trade-offs to consider when using multisig. How many keys should there be (N)? How how many keys should be required to sign (M)? As the number and distribution of keys increases, so does the complexity of maintaining your setup. And as an old security adage goes, complexity is the enemy of security.

As a bit of practical advice, 2-of-3 and 3-of-5 are among the more common multisig wallet setups. But your particular risk tolerance, technical expertise and value at risk should determine which parameters are right for you.

Sovereign HODLing

In this chapter, you learned about the different kinds of wallets from hottest to coldest. We discussed the various pros and cons, and which kinds of wallets serve which kinds of purposes. There is no one-size-fits-all solution for storing your Bitcoin. For most users, having a combination of wallets for different use cases (some for spending and others for HODLing) will make the most sense.

The best way to see how Bitcoin works for you is to get a wallet and try it out yourself. But no matter which kinds of wallets you end up using, make sure you control your own private keys. This is the only way to become a fully sovereign HODLer of your Bitcoin. Not your keys, not your coins.

On this journey of how Bitcoin works for you, we've touched on a number of components of the Bitcoin technology. You've learned how wallets protect users'

private keys and use them to sign and broadcast transactions. You've learned how miners produce blocks and
how full nodes validate that all of the consensus rules
are being followed.

It's time now to step away from the technical side of
Bitcoin and dig into its monetary aspect. In Part III
we'll discuss the monetary properties of Bitcoin which
arise from its unique, trust-minimising architecture.

PART III

What does Bitcoin achieve?

CHAPTER 8

Digital Rivalry and Excludability

This book started with a question: "how can a purely digital money that's not backed by anything have any value to people at all?" By now you've seen how it is the people of Bitcoin who ultimately imbue the project with value.

HODLers and others who run full nodes verify transactions on the network. This protects the integrity of the chain of payments. Miners produce proof of work. The demand for proof of work secures the network against censorship and centralization. Bitcoin's three parts—social, technological and monetary—are mutually reinforcing and inseparable.

Here in Part III, we'll explore the nature of Bitcoin as a monetary good. To best function as money, an economic good should be rival, excludable, fungible and hard. In this chapter we'll talk about the first two properties, rivalry and excludability, leaving the other two for the next chapter.

For all of these properties, we'll discuss how Bitcoin fares compared to gold and to fiat currency (both physical notes/coins and bank account credit). You'll see how Bitcoin is already superior to these other monetary media along most dimensions, and the situation is improving rapidly. Let's start by discussing rivalry and why it's a vital characteristic for good money.

Good Money Must Be Rival

An economic good is *rival* if only one person can have it or enjoy it at a time. By contrast, if a good can be enjoyed by many people simultaneously, then it's *non-rival*.

Monetary goods must be rival. Once you give the money to someone else, you don't still have it, and you can't spend it again. If you could, then this presents a *double-spend problem*—a situation in which the same money can be spent more than once at the same time.

For a physical monetary good, like a gold coin, double-spending is not an issue because the physicality of the object ensures that it is rival. After someone gives you a gold coin, they don't still have it. Likewise, when you hand over the coin to someone else, you no longer have it.

But things get more complicated when instead of spending the thing itself, you spend a promise. While you can't double-spend a physical gold coin, you could pledge the same gold coin more than once. That is, you could issue IOUs against coins you don't have. This introduces trust.

When a physical gold coin changes hands, the transaction settles immediately and so trust is minimised. But when someone accepts your promise to deliver a gold coin, they have to trust that you'll remain solvent and that you'll follow through on delivery. The physicality of gold ensures that it can't be double-spent, but at the same time, it requires physical settlement in order to be trust minimizing. This can be cumbersome since transactors must be in the same place at the same time. If the parties can't transact in person, they can use third party couriers, but this reintroduces trust. Now the trusted third party is the delivery person.

To be trust minimizing, real physical assets require real physical delivery. And moreover, physical goods have to be *assayed*—that is, tested—to ensure their quality. Assaying introduces its own costs, so much so that professionally managed, custodial gold bars (Good Delivery[56] bars) carry a price premium over spot delivered bars. The physicality of real assets makes them difficult to transact trustlessly both for delivery and for quality assurance reasons.

Consequently, the desire to *dematerialize* assets— that is, to exchange digital representations of assets rather than the assets themselves—is a strong one. Unlike physical goods, digital representations of assets can be transacted electronically, at the speed of the Internet. But a digital representation of a real world asset is merely a promise, not the thing itself.

And promises can be double-spent.

Double-spending Promises

In point of fact, the entire legacy financial system is built on the premise that promises can be double-spent, up to a point. Let's explore how.

When you take out a mortgage to buy a house, you pledge the house against the credit that the bank loans to you to buy it. This is called *hypothecation.* Your house is collateral for the loan, and even though you retain ownership, the lien holder (the bank) could seize it if you fail to repay.

Other kinds of assets can be hypothecated too, and frequently are. Securities, for instance, are financial assets (like stocks or bonds) that can be traded and used as collateral for loans. When an asset is pledged as collateral, the receiving lender can sometimes turn around and re-pledge that same security to yet another financial institution for another loan. In this case, the asset has been *rehypothecated*—that is, hypothecated (promised) again.

In the financial world, rehypothecation of assets is common. To entice borrowers to permit their collateral to be rehypothecated, lenders will offer reduced interest rates or other rebates. Collectively, rehypothecation creates *leverage* in the financial system. This means that there are more loans (more credit) than there are assets underlying them.

How much more? That depends on how many times assets have been rehypothecated. In aggregate, this number is called the *churn factor*. The high churn factor in the financial system prior to 2008 has been implicated in the Global Financial Crisis that followed[57].

But it's not just securities that get rehypothecated. Fiat currency itself is a chain of promises.

In a fractional reserve banking system, banks are required to keep only a fraction of depositors' funds on hand. Often this fraction is around 10%. This means that a bank can issue $90 of credit (loans) against a $100 deposit. But in turn, that $90 gets deposited at another bank, which turns around and creates another $81 in loan credit, and so on. Continuing this process, the banking system will have created roughly $1000 in credit against an original deposit of $100. This *money multiplier effect* of fractional reserve banking is the churn factor of fiat currency.

The edifice of modern finance is a tower of promises stacked on promises. Homes are collateral for mortgages. Mortgages are collateral for Mortgage Backed Securities (MBSs). Securities are rehypothecated as Collateralized Debt Obligations (CDOs). Gold bullion is custodially vaulted and securitized into Exchange

Traded Funds (ETFs). Even the money itself (fiat currency) is a chain of promises backed by nothing but debt[58].

As communication technology has improved, the pressure to make assets tradable online has lead to their dematerialization. Instead of exchanging tangible assets, financiers trade digital doppelgängers, virtual ghosts of things of real value. The delivery and performance of these instruments depend on myriad intermediaries, third parties and middle men, many of whom have an incentive to re-pledge the assets and double-spend them. With so many hands on these modern financial instruments, it's hard to make the case that they are rival goods. And without the property of rivalry, they don't make for good money, despite being used as such[59].

To be able to transact online and still enjoy the immediate, final settlement of cash, we need a digitally native, rival good. Enter Bitcoin.

The Birth of Digital Rivalry

Prior to Bitcoin, digital goods were rival only insofar as the various third parties could be trusted not to rehypothecate them. And unfortunately, as we just saw with the legacy financial system, the profit potential of re-pledging assets is too attractive to resist.

Bitcoin gave birth to digital rivalry. Unlike bank account balances or securities, Bitcoin's monetary units —sats—are not promises. They are not claims to any other asset, physical or digital. Each sat is the thing itself.

Secured by proof of work and enshrined in the blockchain, Bitcoin transactions are irreversible. Sats cannot be double-spent. Every full node on the Bitcoin computer network independently verifies the legitimacy of every transaction.

Bitcoin is the first truly rival, digital good, making it an excellent candidate for good money. But this is just one property. Let's see how Bitcoin does on the related property of excludability.

Good Money Must Be Excludable

While rivalry has to do with whether a good can be used simultaneously by more than one person, excludability has to do with how that good is acquired and held.

A good is *excludable* if it's practical to keep people from gaining access to it at will. If it's impossible or impractical to keep others from acquiring the good, then it is *non-excludable*. Once acquired, a monetary good must be excludable. If a holder can't prevent others from accessing it, then it won't make for good money.

It's important here to distinguish between money that is already in circulation vs. the potential future supply. Here we're only interested in the excludability of units in circulation. How money comes into circulation (from the future supply) is the topic of hardness, which we'll cover in the next chapter.

Of the three monetary media we've been discussing —Bitcoin, gold and fiat currency—Bitcoin is the most excludable. Recall that the holder of an amount of Bitcoin is whoever has the private key for that value[60]. This means that any amount of value representable in Bitcoin can be secured with a tiny amount of information (the key). The seed for a Bitcoin wallet fits comfortably on an index card.

Beyond using a single key to secure Bitcoin, holders can employ multi-signature (multisig) wallets[61]. Using multisig, your keys can be kept in separate locations. This makes it more difficult for an attacker who might try to access them, which further increases your security.

What's more, the Bitcoin protocol offers *timelocks*, which can lock up value completely until a future date or block height[62]. Using a timelock, you can make it impossible for your funds to move until some time that you predetermine. Like all spending conditions, timelocks are enforced by every node on the network. This kind of smart contract provides a high degree of security, excluding your funds from access by everyone, even yourself.

Compare these features of Bitcoin to gold bullion or physical fiat currency (notes and coins). Increasing amounts of gold or fiat take up more physical space, increasing the security cost. By contrast, increasing amounts of Bitcoin can be secured using the same 12-24 word seed phrase.

We've talked about Bitcoin, gold and physical fiat currency, but what about bank account credit? A well-functioning monetary media should be excludable, but your bank account can be frozen or your funds seized. Commercial banks are required to report suspicious activity to law enforcement[63]. Bank records are sometimes used to carry out immigration checks[64]. With respect to excludability, Bank account balances are the worst.

For these reasons, Bitcoin is the closest thing we have to an *unconfiscatable* monetary good. Of course it's still possible for an attacker to threaten a Bitcoin holder in many ways (bodily harm, blackmail, kidnapping, etc.) But this misses the point. No matter what other factors are brought to bear, if the keys are secure, it is only by the holder's action that the Bitcoin value can be moved. No power on Earth can confiscate a key holder's Bitcoin without their compliance.

Bitcoin is Superior

In this chapter, you saw how Bitcoin is the first and most rival/excludable digital good. Bitcoin does not depend on a centralized third party for clearing, which minimizes trust when transacting. An amount of Bitcoin in the circulating supply is a rival and excludable bearer asset.

Meanwhile, the legacy financial system is digital insofar as assets have been replaced by electronic claims on them. To expedite trade, traditional assets have been dematerialized. They're exchanged and cleared through third parties who have every incentive to rehypothecate them. This exposes holders to counterparty risk and dilution of value. Legacy finance is a tower of promises stacked on promises.

Bitcoin is superior to both fiat currency and gold in terms of rivalry and excludability. But what about other important properties of good money, like fungibility and hardness? We'll dive into these properties next.

CHAPTER 9

Fungibility and Hardness

Last chapter, we discussed how Bitcoin is the first digital, rival, excludable good. These properties are necessary for being good money, but they're not the end of the story. In this chapter we'll discuss two other desirable properties for good money: fungibility and hardness.

Just like last chapter, we'll describe these properties and we'll evaluate how Bitcoin stands up against traditional monetary media (gold and fiat currency). You'll see that on fungibility, Bitcoin is a competitor. While there's room for improvement, new developments on the horizon are likely to make the situation better. But on hardness, there is no competition. Bitcoin is the hardest money ever conceived.

Let's talk about fungibility first.

Good Money is Fungible

Money is a tool to facilitate human cooperation and coordination by transferring value across time and distance. It satisfies our human need for reciprocity, encoding debt obligations in transferable, unitized form[65].

This works best when monetary units are interchangeable with one another. Ideally, a monetary good's units should be indistinguishable. That way, measuring value is reduced to a counting problem.

An economic good is *fungible* in the degree to which recipients don't care which particular instance of that good they receive. In a word, fungible goods are interchangeable. Fungibility is desirable because it makes exchange reliable and rapid, and it makes value computation easy.

To this end, there are two factors that contribute to the fungibility of a monetary good: the uniformity of its units in the present, and the memory of its units through time. Let's discuss each of these factors as they apply to gold, then to fiat currency and finally to Bitcoin.

Fungibility of Gold

Gold serves as a store of value worldwide, maintaining a significant monetary premium over its value as an industrial material. But when you receive gold, how do you know that it's gold that you're getting?

Coins and bars minted by reputable producers typically have markings denoting their origin and quality, but these could be faked. In the gold bullion trade, high-value bars are vaulted and custodied to ensure uniform quality[66]. But even so, bars in some the world's biggest banks have been found to be counterfeit. These sophisticated forgeries carry the stamps of Swiss refineries, but come from parts unknown[67].

Due to the expense of verifying both the quality and the history of gold bullion, this task ends up being concentrated into a small number of firms who become trusted third parties. And as we've discussed at some length, introducing trusted third parties sacrifices other properties of good money (rivalry and excludability).

So gold can be fungible, but only insofar as it can be reliably assayed or its custodians trusted. How fungible is fiat currency?

Fungibility of Fiat Currency

For a sovereign fiat currency, all physical units are of identical quality by decree. This is what legal tender laws are for. By law, an offer of physical fiat currency is declared to be good for discharging all debts public and private. Creditors are obliged to accept their local fiat currency at par value (face value) for payment of outstanding debts. (Technically speaking, a creditor can refuse the cash offer, but the debt is legally cancelled just the same).

Even so, not all physical fiat currency is equally desirable despite having the same face value. In China and other parts of Asia, it's customary to give gifts of money in decorative envelopes. For gifting, only clean, new notes will do[68]. And around the world, collectors preserve coins and notes for their numismatic value.

From a fungibility perspective, it would be convenient to disregard bank credit and focus solely on physical currency units. But this would be disingenuous. The physical currency component of the U.S. money supply represents less than 11.2% of the total[69], most of which is overseas[70]. Globally, only around 8.4% of world money supply exists in physical currency form[71]. So roughly 90% of all fiat currency exists only as bank credit.

Jurisdictions differ on whether bank account credit counts as legal tender, but in most places it does not. This means that while creditors may choose to accept bank account credit (cheques, credit cards) as payment, they are under no obligation to do so.

Merchants may require a surcharge from customers paying with credit, or offer cash discounts. It makes sense for merchants to do this because credit payments come with the risk of *chargeback*, a practice wherein the crediting institution takes the payment back from the merchant (for example if the customer disputed the charge). Chargebacks eat into merchants' profit margins, and having too many of them can trigger expensive penalties from payment processors[72].

Because of chargeback risk, not all fiat payment systems are equal. A dollar paid through one mechanism is not as desirable as one paid through another mechanism. So while fiat currency is supposed to be fungible by force of law, in practice it is less than perfect. Most fiat exists in the form of bank credit, and transfers are mediated by payment processors. These intermediaries introduce chargeback risk and they prevent fiat currency from operating as a pure, fungible, bearer asset.

Now let's talk about the fungibility of Bitcoin.

Fungibility of Bitcoin

Unlike gold, which has to be assayed for quality, Bitcoin's monetary units don't have this problem. Each sat is perfect and identical to all others in much the same way that gold atoms are[73]. This is because sats are commingled in unspent transaction outputs (UTXOs). With each transaction, it is as though the sats are melted down and recast. Every full node on the network independently validates every transaction, guaranteeing the quality of all sats.

However, the full transparency of transactions afforded by the blockchain has a drawback. While it guarantees the quality of sats, it also preserves their history, which can hurt fungibility.

Once a Bitcoin address is associated with a particular real-world entity, market participants could choose not to perform Bitcoin transactions that involve that address. For example, in November, 2018, the U.S. Department of the Treasury's Office of Foreign Assets

Control (OFAC) published two Bitcoin addresses connected with Iran-based individuals subject to sanctions[74]. Regulated U.S. actors could be subject to secondary sanctions if they are caught sending funds to these addresses[75].

Whenever a money is traceable by authorities, it creates a demand for money laundering services. *Money laundering* is the act of concealing or obfuscating the path of payments of criminal origin. Holders of dirty money exchange it for clean money through a money launderer, who assumes the risk associated with handling the dirty funds for a fee.

To the degree that Bitcoin can be used for money laundering, this takes two forms. First, simply by using Bitcoin at all, this increases the number of systems a future investigator would have to traverse to follow the money. Generally this is a bad idea for the would-be launderer, though, because all transactions are transparent on the blockchain. Nonetheless, using Bitcoin in this way can be significantly cheaper than traditional fiat money laundering services[76].

The second way Bitcoin can be used for money laundering is through the coinbase transaction produced during the mining process. By mining for Bitcoin, someone can spend dirty money on electricity and produce detached (clean) Bitcoin[77]. This works even if the network difficulty is too high to make mining a profitable business in its own right. The difference between the cost paid in electricity and the price received at market for the Bitcoin is the cost of doing business.

Setting up and running a miner is a pretty heavyweight process for obfuscating the source of non-Bitcoin funds. But what about amounts that are already in Bitcoin? To disrupt chain analysis—which can track Bitcoin amounts through the transactions in the blockchain—users can employ a technique called a *CoinJoin*. In a CoinJoin, users work together to build a single transaction with many inputs and many outputs. This helps to break the association between inputs and outputs since it wouldn't be clear to an outside observer whose outputs belong to whom[78].

While privacy-oriented wallets have made it relatively easy to engage in CoinJoin transactions, it's still an extra step. Users who want to take advantage of this privacy feature have to explicitly opt in by running a compatible wallet, engaging in CoinJoin transactions, and paying both the Bitcoin mining fees and any CoinJoin coordination fees.

Another way Bitcoiners can enhance their privacy is to use the Lightning Network to route payments instead of performing transactions directly on chain. The Lighting Network is a second layer technology that uses Bitcoin transactions to settle. It facilitates rapid payments by updating balances in what are called Payment Channels, which are like shared accounts. Only the transactions to open and close Payment Channels are committed to the global public ledger. Incremental payments that are made through the Lightning Network are near-instantaneous and leave no outwardly visible trail.

Lastly, several improvements to the Bitcoin protocol itself are currently being developed that will increase privacy—and thus fungibility—on chain. They go by strange names like Merkelized Abstract Syntax Trees (MAST), Schnorr signatures and Taproot. Once implemented, these techniques will make possible more complex, multi-party Bitcoin contracts that look to outside observers just like regular payments[79].

So while Bitcoin has not historically been perfectly fungible due to its global, public ledger, the situation is improving. It's reasonable to expect that ongoing enhancements to both the core protocols and second layer technologies will continue to increase the privacy and fungibility of Bitcoin over time.

Of gold, fiat currency and Bitcoin, none are perfectly fungible. But while the fungibility of gold and fiat currency seem to be getting worse (more intermediaries with increased oversight), the fungibility of Bitcoin is improving both with the adoption of second layer technologies and with the development of updates to the underlying Bitcoin protocols.

Bitcoin is not yet the clear winner on fungibility, but it is already the hardest money yet conceived. Let's discuss why this is, and why hardness matters in the next section.

The Hardest Money Ever Conceived

In monetary terms, the hardness of a good is a description of how difficult it is to introduce more of it into circulation[80]. Sometimes people mistake the term hardness to mean physical durability (the opposite of soft). But for money, the opposite of hard is easy. The harder the money, the more work has to be put into circulating additional units.

Physical durability has often contributed to monetary hardness in our species' history. For example, the early inhabitants of North America used shell beads for money called wampum. To them, wampum was hard money. It could only be produced near the ocean, where the mollusks grew, and each bead took human labor to produce. Because of this, only a small number of tribes specialized in its production, and yet the beads traded far inland[81].

But eventually, when colonists introduced industrial manufacturing techniques, wampum went from being hard money to being easy money. Overproduction destroyed the value of existing wampum, and with it, the wealth of its holders.

For something to function as good money, and to satisfy our need for reciprocity, it has to be hard. Anything that's easily produced will tend to be overproduced in response to increasing demand. Good money should have a stubborn supply. It should resist increases in demand.

To this end, Bitcoin is the hardest money ever conceived. Its total amount is not just slow to grow, but ultimately and unwaveringly fixed. ₿21 million is all that there will ever be, and they are produced on a predictable and unalterable schedule. The consensus rules of Bitcoin production are enforced independently by each and every full node on the network. With every additional HODLer, the permanence of the Bitcoin supply cap is further cemented and assured.

When the price of Bitcoin goes up (as measured in fiat currency), the profitability of mining Bitcoin also increases. This incentives miners to expand operations, converting more electricity into cryptographic hashes. When miners increase their efforts, blocks are produced more quickly than the 10 minute target, so for a little while, Bitcoin is produced faster. But, in response to the faster block time, the network of Bitcoin full nodes increases the required difficulty to compensate.

This automatic, global *difficulty retargeting*, is the key technical innovation to preserving Bitcoin's issuance schedule. Bringing new industrial techniques to bear on Bitcoin mining cannot increase the total future supply of Bitcoin, and it can only temporarily speed up its issuance. In other words, no amount of industrial effort can destroy the value held by Bitcoin HODLers like it did for holders of wampum.

Even gold is not as hard as Bitcoin. Each year, about 1-2% more gold is mined and added to the global stock. In 2018, for example, about 1.7% was added[82]. Although supply of new gold fluctuates from year to year, it has increased steadily over time in response to demand. When demand for gold increases, so does its price, and miners go to work producing more. The total stock of above ground gold increases exponentially over time (1-2% annually).

There is no practical limit to the amount of gold that could be produced. And we're not even limited to only the gold ore trapped in the Earth's crust. NASA is planning a mission to investigate a metallic asteroid called 16 Psyche[83] that is estimated to contain many times more gold than has been mined so far on Earth[84].

There are asteroids filled with gold, but there are no asteroids filled with Bitcoin.

Becoming World Money

Between this chapter and the previous, we've explored how Bitcoin fares against gold and fiat currency considering the monetary properties of rivalry, excludability, fungibility and hardness. In most of these ways, Bitcoin is already the superior monetary medium, and where it isn't, the situation is improving.

It would be fair for a critic to point out, though, that these are not the only properties that matter in monetary media. We haven't discussed liquidity, transaction costs, and network effects to name just a few examples. While these and other properties are certainly important, the four we've covered over the last two chapters are vital:

- To function as money, a good must be rival and excludable once acquired. Bitcoin is the first and most rival/excludable, digital good.

- To enable rapid and reliable trade, monetary units must be fungible. Bitcoin's fungibility leaves something to be desired because the history of transactions is explorable on the blockchain. But second layer technologies and protocol upgrades are making this better.

- To satisfy our need for reciprocity, and to transfer value across time and distance, a monetary good must be hard. Bitcoin is the hardest money ever made.

As a monetary medium, Bitcoin has all the properties necessary to become world money. That is, to become the way we secure and measure intersubjective value. Next, in the final chapter of the book, let's explore a new function of money that Bitcoin could fulfill at saturation: a global metric for expressing intersubjective value. We'll conclude with a look at the road ahead.

CHAPTER 10
Metric of Intersubjective Value

The reason that Bitcoin has value to anyone at all is that it is good money. As a monetary good, sats (Bitcoin's units) are rival, excludable once obtained, and mostly fungible—a situation that's improving day by day. Issuance of sats is an equal opportunity enterprise (anyone can mine Bitcoin), and yet the total supply is ultimately fixed. Bitcoin is the hardest, fairest money ever conceived.

On top of that, Bitcoin is digitally native and inherently global. Bitcoin is borderless. Every person who runs a full node independently verifies the consensus rules, ensuring that no one can cheat the system. In a world of increasing privacy concerns, Bitcoin transactions are uncensorable and pseudonymous.

Having answered the core question at the heart of this book, we could stop our journey here. You've learned how Bitcoin is three things: a social phenomenon, a computer network and a programmable money. You've seen how these social, technological and monetary parts fit together and how each part operates by consensus. You've also learned the basics of how Bitcoin works for you and how its vital monetary properties arise from its design.

But is that all there is to the story? Here in the final chapter of the book, let's peer forward at what Bitcoin could become as more people learn the Value of Bitcoin. This is where we depart from simply describing the status quo, and instead speculate about the future.

In short, I predict that at saturation, Bitcoin will become a global metric of intersubjective value. Everything that can be measured in sats will come to be measured in sats. You may think this sounds crazy. Let me explain.

First, we need to talk about the kinds of things that people buy and how we typically express value measurements for them. We'll discuss consumption purchases at small and large scale. Then we'll talk about low risk assets, and finally investments. You'll see that the metrics that we use to express value depend on the types of things being purchased, and what they're being purchased for.

With this framing in place, we'll explore the role that sats would play in a Bitcoin saturated future. Some everyday items might still be priced in local fiat currency units. And some investments would still be measured against industry benchmarks. But for the vast area in between, I predict that the opportunity cost of not holding Bitcoin will be the measure of the value of other things.

We'll conclude the book by looking to what would need to occur for this to take place. And, perhaps more importantly, what would be different in the world if it does.

Measuring Value

How do you measure value? We use length units like meters to measure distances. We use time units like seconds to measure durations. But what units do you use to measure the value of something?

While objects' physical properties (like length) are objectively, scientifically measurable, an object's value is thoroughly subjective[85]. Value, like beauty, is in the eye of the beholder. We can objectively measure the duration of a sunset. But its beauty—its value—is appraised subjectively by those who experience it.

There are many things in life, like sunsets, for which we might struggle to attach a price. But for those things that we can price, we tend to measure and communicate their value in different ways depending on the context.

Of the things that are available to buy, let's group them into strata and then talk about how people tend to measure the value of each. That will lead us into a discussion of how Bitcoin fits in. These strata are:

- Small scale consumer purchases — Everyday items, consumables, food, clothing. Things you use up.

- Large scale consumer purchases — Middle class liabilities like a car or home[86].

- Low risk assets — Money-market accounts, government debt in the form of bonds, some kinds of real estate, some commodities (precious metals).

- Investments — Capital assets, debt instruments and equity (both public and private).

While you might think that people use currency to measure the value of all of these things, in practice each of these strata may use different units for assessing value and for carrying out transactions. Let's start with small scale purchases and work our way up.

Small Scale Consumer Purchases

Metric: Local fiat currency.

In the course of everyday living, we use things up. Toothpaste, water, food, clothing. Once used, these items lose all or most of their value. They become garbage after use. Economists refer to these as *non-durable* goods or *consumables.*

When pricing these goods, the unit of account is typically the local fiat currency. In the U.S., people earn and spend U.S. dollars (USD). In India, they earn and spend Indian rupees. In Japan, people earn and spend Japanese yen, and so on.

Large Scale Consumer Purchases

Metric: Hard money.

Beyond small purchases, we have large scale consumer purchases. These include vehicles (cars, trucks, boats) and homes used as a principal residence (apartments, condominiums, houses). Like smaller purchases, these things get used up. They degrade due to wear and tear. But they retain more value than their smaller scale cousins. They are *durable* goods.

In some places, these larger scale consumables are priced in the same units as smaller scale consumer purchases. For example, in the U.S., one would expect to find both cars and the gasoline to fuel them priced in USD.

But in other places, you'll find that the more expensive items are priced in a unit other than the local fiat currency. In Argentina, even though people earn and spend Argentine pesos, USD is often used to price large items such as real estate[87]. As the size of the purchase increases, it's more likely that the seller will measure its value in the harder, more stable money.

Low Risk Assets

Metric: Risk-free rate.

Next we have low risk assets. While both small and large scale purchases are expected to provide some use value to the buyer, low risk assets are primarily acquired for their ability to store value.

Physical cash is perhaps the canonical low risk asset because, as the saying goes, cash is king. No matter what the market thinks of your other goods, people will still accept your cash. Cash is liquid.

But fiat cash does not offer any kind of return. And it depreciates due to price inflation. For this reason, people who have wealth to store typically don't keep the bulk of it in physical fiat currency. To escape inflation, people sometimes buy non-perishable, hard collectibles like gold. Sometimes the very wealthy buy art and real estate in desirable locations[88].

But precious metals, art, and real estate expose the buyer to price risk. There's variability in the prices these things fetch at market over time. So instead, people sometimes buy other low risk assets like money market accounts or government debt (bonds) which offer a small nominal rate of interest.

Here we need to distinguish between price and value. The prices of assets are often denominated in fiat units. But their value to a portfolio is not so straightforward because portfolios have to forecast changes over time. A portfolio manager can't focus exclusively on current spot prices or instruments' face values.

Financial planners and economists compare the return on assets against what's called the *risk-free rate of return*. This is the expected return of a hypothetical investment with zero risk. Although there are many kinds of risk, in this context risk means volatility or variance in the return[89].

While a truly risk-free rate doesn't exist, the nearest proxy is usually the yield of a government bond over the period of inquiry[90]. In times of relative regime stability, this makes sense. A nation that issues its own currency is never at risk of defaulting on its debts denominated in same. The sovereign can always create currency to service any debt[91].

Over the recent historical period, the interest offered by government debt is widely regarded the lowest risk interest rate available. For this reason, stores of value are often measured against this low risk rate.

Investments

Metric: Industry benchmark rate.

Lastly, let's talk about investments. Beyond simple storage of value, an investor wants to make a superlative return. If you buy a gold coin, you don't expect it to do anything. It is what it is. But when you buy a share of stock, you expect the company to produce something of value to the market. When you buy a corporate bond, you expect the company to pay down the debt plus interest out of its earnings.

There are lots of ways to invest. How do people choose among them?

Modern Portfolio Theory takes for granted that investors want to receive a return on their investment and are willing to tolerate some amount of risk to get it. Returns are good. Variability (risk) is bad. Given expectations about the returns and volatility of various investments, you can construct a portfolio that maximizes your return for your particular level of risk tolerance[92].

But dealing with two variables (risk and reward) is complicated. To simplify things, analysts often combine the two into a single *risk-adjusted rate of return*. For example, dividing the expected return by the variance gives you a metric called the Sharpe ratio[93]. Funds with higher Sharpe ratios offer higher returns for the level of risk assumed compared to the risk-free rate.

But is the risk-free rate a good enough baseline? Over the last few decades, investment has increasingly shifted away from actively managed funds and toward passively managed funds[94]. In actively managed funds, managers make investment decisions on behalf of holders. While in passively managed funds, investment decisions are algorithmically determined, for example to track an index like the S&P 500.

Rather than being compared to the risk-free rate, active portfolio managers are now often judged against passive portfolios. In equity investing, for instance, the benchmark is often the S&P, standing as a proxy for the market as a whole. The index is the benchmark against which other strategies are measured.

Now that we've talked about the four strata of things people buy, let's recap how different metrics are used for each.

Different Metrics for Different Purposes

In the previous section, we talked about four different strata of things people buy, and we looked at the metrics people use to express their value. To review: Small scale consumer purchases are typically priced in the local fiat currency. These items get used up and become garbage afterward.

Large scale consumer purchases retain some value after use. You can resell your used furniture or your vehicles. You may even expect your home to appreciate if you live in an improving area. The larger the purchase, the more likely that the seller will express its price in better money. In places with strong currencies, it may be the same local fiat units as smaller purchases. But the worse the local currency is at holding value, the more likely it'll be abandoned for better money when pricing larger items.

While large consumer items have some capacity to store value, low risk assets are purchased primarily for that purpose. Gold, art and real estate expose the buyer to market price risk, but protect against price inflation compared to holding fiat. Other low risk assets like government debt offer a nominal rate of interest and serve as a baseline for measuring the profitability of other instruments.

At the highest level of risk and reward, investors purchase productive assets to achieve a return. For them, a more aggressive but variable baseline makes sense. Often, they'll compare returns against an index like the S&P 500.

In terms of their effect on value, these four strata run the gamut of totally consumptive (small scale purchases) to totally productive (investments). In between, we have things that mostly store value but may have some consumptive or productive value (large scale purchases and low risk assets respectively). To see this all laid out graphically, take a look at the following diagram:

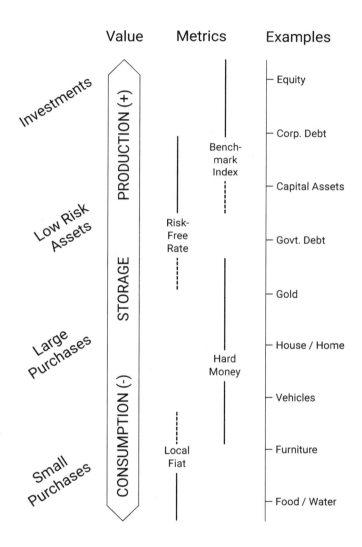

Today: Strata of things people buy, their relationship to value, the metrics we use to express value, and examples.

This diagram is arranged in four columns. The first column lists the four strata that we've been discussing. From bottom to top: small scale consumer purchases, large scale consumer purchases, low risk assets and investments. To the right of that, in the second column, is a value scale with consumption at the bottom, storage in the middle and production at the top.

The third column shows the metrics: local fiat currency, hard money, the risk-free rate, and the benchmark index. Each metric is drawn as a vertical line. The position and height of each line shows roughly what it is used to measure on the value scale. These lines overlap somewhat because people make their own decisions about which metric to use in different places and in various situations. The fourth and final column lists some example items for reference.

So far so good. In this section we've laid out the kinds of things people buy, their relation to value, and the metrics we currently use to measure and express that value. Now let's use this framing to imagine what role Bitcoin would play at saturation.

Bitcoin at Saturation

In this section, we'll consider the role that Bitcoin would have in expressing value in a future where it is widely desired. I call this *saturation*.

There's no specific adoption measurement attached to this term—it's intentionally hand-wavy. What I mean is that, at saturation, most people in most places will know what Bitcoin is and would be happy to have some sats. Much like gold or U.S. dollars are today.

If you're saying to yourself "that's ridiculous", that's OK. The point of this exercise is to imagine how things would be different if it came to pass. For now, I hope you'll go with it.

OK, so we're imagining that Bitcoin has reached saturation. HODLers are abundant, and people worldwide know what Bitcoin is. Most people are still compensated for their labor in local fiat currency, but they're happy to work for sats if they find the opportunity. It's relatively easy to switch between Bitcoin and local fiat currency at a low cost. People use their Bitcoin balances and local fiat balances much like a savings account and a checking account respectively.

As we discussed in the preceding chapter, Bitcoin is the hardest money ever conceived. So in a Bitcoin saturated future, large scale consumer purchases (cars, houses) would naturally be priced in Bitcoin. People would still price pure consumables (food, water) in local fiat currency, but goods which have the ability to store value have to compete with holding Bitcoin. The price of any large scale purchase is the opportunity cost of not holding the same balance in sats.

So the role of hard money would go to Bitcoin. But what about the risk-free rate? Would we still use the yield of government bonds to evaluate other low risk assets?

No. In a Bitcoin saturated future, the risk-free rate is zero. Zero percent in Bitcoin terms that is. Holding your own private keys to your own sat balances is the lowest risk option. Anyone, even a government, that offers a positive return in Bitcoin terms is asking you to lend them your sats. You lend them only by assuming a number of risks. Will the debtor be able to pay you back (solvency risk)? What if the debtor absconds with the funds (fraud risk)?

The legacy financial system is riddled with middlemen who can intervene and undo transactions. But Bitcoin transactions are final. So while you might be able to buy insurance against fraud (at some cost), as soon as someone else has your Bitcoin, your funds are at risk. The risk-free rate in a Bitcoin saturated future is zero.

Now, of course, there will still be investments. Some people will use some of their sats to purchase debt, equity or capital assets. These investors will want to realize a return for their efforts—some positive amount of Bitcoin above what they put in. By aggregating the results of many such attempts at profit, industry- and economy-wide benchmark returns could be calculated. These indices (specified in Bitcoin terms, and factoring in variance) would be the baselines against which specific investment opportunities would be judged.

But unlike today, where fiat currency price inflation forces everyone to become an investor, in a Bitcoin future, only a portion of folks would take on investment risk. And that's OK. We have been conditioned to chase returns—to make our money work for us—because fiat currency is bad. In a Bitcoin future of good money, we will be released from this pressure. We can choose to step off the treadmill and rest.

Today, we're acclimated to prices increasing over time in fiat terms. This is the scourge of price inflation caused by expansion of the money supply. By contrast, Bitcoin's total future supply is known and fixed. ₿21 million is all there can ever be.

Expressed in sats, prices of things would generally, naturally fall over time, roughly in step with improvements to productivity. This is good. It means that the value that you earn and save in Bitcoin buys you more over time, not less. Saving for retirement will be an achievable goal. And you won't have to gamble on the stock market to do it.

Both the role of hard money and the role of risk-free rate would be subsumed by Bitcoin at saturation. Local fiat currency and benchmark indices would still be used at the edges for small purchases and investments respectively. Plugging Bitcoin into the 'metrics' column of the diagram from the last section gives us the following, updated diagram:

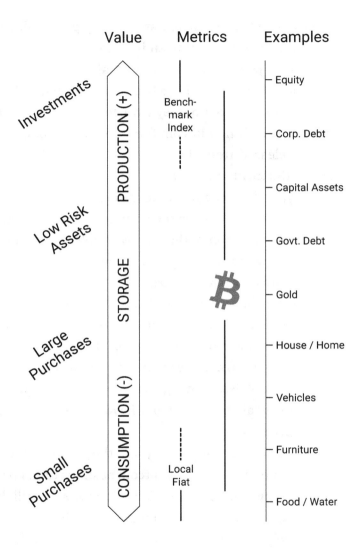

Prediction: At saturation, Bitcoin will become the dominant metric for measuring and expressing intersubjective value.

At the highest level, comparing among investment opportunities, portfolio managers will use available benchmarks. Those benchmarks will be couched as percentage gains in Bitcoin terms, and factor in variance.

At the lowest scale, people will still use their local fiat currency to price purely consumptive goods. That is, as long as States continue to issue and demand their own currency in payment for taxes.

How long people use their local fiat currency to express prices is a function of how strong and stable the local currency is. The weaker the local currency, the more thoroughly people will abandon it for Bitcoin. This is analogous to Argentina today. Because the Argentine peso weakens predictably over time relative to the U.S. dollar, people use the latter to price goods that store value. Likewise, all fiat currencies predictably weaken over time relative to Bitcoin. And at saturation, everyone will know it.

The Rest of the Journey

Back to reality. For Bitcoin to arise as the dominant, global metric of intersubjective value, a lot of things have to take place. It won't happen overnight, and it raises a number of questions.

First, how can we be sure that Bitcoin won't just disappear or become supplanted by something else? Variants of this question include: Can't the government shut Bitcoin down? What if they make it illegal? What stops some other cryptocurrency from replacing Bitcoin? What if the government makes their own cryptocurrency?

These are all good questions. Answering them requires digging further into the social, technological and monetary parts of Bitcoin. It also requires exploring more of the social, technological and monetary environments in which Bitcoin operates. All of this is the subject of the next book in the series.

But the questions don't stop there. Supposing that Bitcoin manages to survive, how much would its units be worth in the long term (the lowercase 'v' value of Bitcoin)? What will your sats be able to buy if Bitcoin becomes the dominant, global metric for expressing intersubjective value? To answer this, we have to estimate the value available to store and project growth going forward.

Lastly, and perhaps most importantly, what will be the far reaching effects of Bitcoin on the future organization of human affairs (the capital 'V' Value of Bitcoin)? How would life be different for people? What effect will Bitcoin have on the economy? On the environment? These are by far the most speculative questions. And the most consequential.

The good news is that we have plenty of time to sort it all out. Bitcoin is only in its second decade, and still below the radar. I look forward to seeing you in the next book, as we continue to map out the Value of Bitcoin.

Acknowledgment

This book went through many revisions and rewrites on its way to you. I am grateful for the readers whose feedback helped to hone this message.

Michael Terry, Netta P. and Tom Brubaker have all been instrumental in shaping this book. Thank you for painstakingly reading and rereading, and for your insightful suggestions. Tars Cunha, thank you for designing a cover that speaks to the brand. People absolutely do judge books by their covers.

I'd also like to thank these folks for their editorial critique and support. In alphabetical order: AG070, Alex (@itsminawhile), Andrei, Anton Livaja, CanEx, Coinicarus, Dan Barrett, Erich, Grumpy, Jim Wilson (Eagertask), Jordan (Greenhall) Hall, Junjay Tan, Kevin Gao, Leffe, Miguel Ariza, My_Livin_Truth, Raheem, Ricardo, Saint Bitcoin, S3, Tareef Kawaf. This book would not have been as good without you.

I'm grateful for my family, who has put up with my Bitcoin obsession these many years. I love you.

Lastly, I'm grateful for the plebs—those humble, toxic, pseudonymous defenders of Bitcoin, its sociological immune system. May your tacos be bountiful and your keys be safe. Thanks.

Notes and References

1. Buxton, Bill. *The Long Nose of Innovation.* Business Week, January 2, 2008 (Revised May 30, 2014).

   https://www.billbuxton.com/01%20The%20Long%20Nose%20o f%20Innovation%20Revised.pdf

2. Nakamoto, Satoshi. *Bitcoin: A Peer-to-Peer Electronic Cash System.* October 31, 2008.

   https://bitcoin.org/bitcoin.pdf

3. Bitcoin's genesis block was mined by Satoshi Nakamoto and recorded on January 3, 2009.

   Its hash is `000000000019d6689c085ae165831e934ff76 3ae46a2a6c172b3f1b60a8ce26f`

4. Nakamoto, Satoshi. *New icon/logo.* Bitcoin Forum, February 24, 2010.

   https://bitcointalk.org/index.php?topic=64

5. Wilson, Phil. *Bitcoin Symbol and Logo Origins.* March 27, 2017.

   https://medium.com/@_Phil_Wilson_/bitcoin-symbol-and-logo-o rigins-5d428d40380

6. Antonopoulos, Andreas M. *Mastering Bitcoin 2nd Edition - Programming the Open Blockchain.* 2018.

   https://github.com/bitcoinbook/bitcoinbook

7. Dunbar, Charles F. "Deposits as Currency." *Quarterly Journal of Economics, Vol. 1, No. 4,* July, 1887. pp. 401-419.

    https://www.jstor.org/stable/i332259

8. Engemann, Kristie. "The Fed's Inflation Target: Why 2 Percent?" *Open Vault Blog,* Federal Reserve Bank of St. Louis, January 16, 2019.

    https://www.stlouisfed.org/open-vault/2019/january/fed-inflation -target-2-percent

9. "The definition of price stability." European Central Bank website, Retrieved May 5, 2020.

    https://www.ecb.europa.eu/mopo/strategy/pricestab/html/index.e n.html

10. "India adopts inflation target of 4% for next five years under monetary policy framework." *The Economic Times,* August 6, 2016.

    https://economictimes.indiatimes.com/articleshow/53564923.cms

11. Pinker, Steven. *Enlightenment Now: The Case for Reason, Science, Humanism, and Progress.* Viking, 2018.

    See Chapter 8. Wealth, Chapter 9. Inequality and Chapter 17. Quality of Life.

    https://stevenpinker.com/publications/enlightenment-now-case-r eason-science-humanism-and-progress

12. McLeay, Michael; Radia, Amar; and Thomas, Ryland. "Money creation in the modern economy." *Bank of England Quarterly Report, Q1,* 2014.

    https://www.bankofengland.co.uk/-/media/boe/files/quarterly-bu lletin/2014/money-creation-in-the-modern-economy.pdf

13. Ruml, Beardsley. "Taxes for Revenue Are Obsolete." *American Affairs*, January, 1946.

    https://www.constitution.org/tax/us-ic/cmt/ruml_obsolete.pdf

14. Wray, L. Randall. "What Are Taxes For? The MMT Approach." *New Economic Perspectives*, May 15, 2014.

    http://neweconomicperspectives.org/2014/05/taxes-mmt-approach.html

15. "Consumer Price Index." Bureau of Labor Statistics website, Retrieved May 5, 2020.

    https://www.bls.gov/cpi/

16. Simmel, Georg; Frisby, David. *The Philosophy of Money*. Routledge, 2004, pp. 508-509.

    http://www.eddiejackson.net/web_documents/Philosophy%20of%20Money.pdf

17. Woods, Thomas E. "Meltdown: a free-market look at why the stock market collapsed, the economy tanked, and the government bailout will make things worse." *Regnery Pub.*, 2009, pp. 66-70.

    https://tomwoods.com/book/meltdown/

18. Polleit, Thorsten. "The Cure (Low Interest Rates) Is the Disease." *Mises Daily Articles*, April 5, 2011.

    https://mises.org/library/cure-low-interest-rates-disease

19. Hülsmann, Jörg Guido. *The Ethics of Money Production.* Ludwig Von Mises Institute, 2008.

Hülsmann describes how fiat currency creates moral hazard by its mere existence, then enumerates the myriad effects of this moral hazard on government, business and society. See Part 2, particularly Chapters 12 and 13.

https://mises.org/library/ethics-money-production

20. Hirschman, Albert O. *Exit, Voice, and Loyalty.* Harvard University Press, 1970.

https://www.hup.harvard.edu/catalog.php?isbn=9780674276604

21. Ferdman, Roberto A. "Argentina's insatiable—and destructive—appetite for U.S. dollars." *The Washington Post,* July 31, 2014.

https://www.washingtonpost.com/news/wonk/wp/2014/07/31/argentinas-insatiable-and-destructive-appetite-for-u-s-dollars/

22. Paul, Ron. *End the Fed.* Grand Central Publishing, September 16, 2009.

https://www.grandcentralpublishing.com/titles/ron-paul/end-the-fed/9780446568180/

23. Fleming, Andrew, "Adbusters sparks Wall Street protest." *Vancouver Courier,* September 27, 2011.

https://www.vancourier.com/news/adbusters-sparks-wall-street-protest-1.374299

24. "Federal Reserve Global Phonecast" OccupyWallStreet website, November 9, 2011.

http://occupywallst.org/article/federal-reserve-global-phonecast/

25. Krugman, Paul. "A Skeptic's View of Crypto (from the Point of View of Monetary Economics)." 'Let's Settle This' debate (hosted by Versus by KIO Networks in Mexico City), September, 2018.

    https://youtu.be/Y_IYGeZLLhI

26. Melis, Alicia P. and Semmann, Dirk. "How is human cooperation different?" *Philosophical Transactions of The Royal Society* **365**, 2010, pp. 2663-2674.

    This excellent review paper contains an approachable yet comprehensive summary of the literature on human and non-human cooperation as observed in natural and laboratory settings.

    https://royalsocietypublishing.org/doi/full/10.1098/rstb.2010.0157

27. Trivers, Robert L. "The Evolution of Reciprocal Altruism." *Quarterly Review of Biology*, 1971, 46:35-57.

    http://www.jstor.org/stable/2822435

28. Hartshorne, H., and May, M. A. *Studies in the Nature of Character. Vol. 1, Studies in Deceit; Vol. 2, Studies in Self-Conrol; Vol. 3, Studies in the Organization of Character.* Macmillan N.Y., 1928-1930.

29. Ariely, Dan. *The (Honest) Truth About Dishonesty: How We Lie to Everyone—Especially Ourselves.* Harper, 2012.

    http://danariely.com/books/the-honest-truth-about-dishonesty/

30. Dreber, A., Rand, D. G., Fudenberg, D. & Nowak, M. A. "Winners don't punish." *Nature*, **452**, 2008, pp. 348-351.

    https://www.nature.com/articles/nature06723

31. Krebs, D. L. "Altruism: An examination of the concept and a review of the literature." *Psychological Bulletin*, **73(4)**, 1970, pp. 258-302.

    http://dx.doi.org/10.1037/h0028987

32. Haidt, Jonathan and Joseph, Craig. "The Moral Mind: How Five Sets of Innate Intuitions Guide the Development of Many Culture-Specific Virtues, and Perhaps Even Modules." *The Innate Mind, Volume 3, Foundations and the Future*, 3, 2008.

    https://www.oxfordscholarship.com/view/10.1093/acprof:oso/9780195332834.001.0001/acprof-9780195332834-chapter-19

33. Moral Foundations Theory website. Retrieved May 5, 2020.

    https://moralfoundations.org/

34. "Principles of Persuasion." Influence At Work website, Retrieved May 5, 2020.

    https://www.influenceatwork.com/principles-of-persuasion/

35. Cialdini, Robert. *Influence: The Psychology of Persuasion, Revised Edition*. Harper Collins, 2006.

    https://www.harpercollins.com/9780061241895/influence/

36. Szabo, Nick. *Shelling Out: The Origins of Money*. Satoshi Nakamoto Institute, 2002.

    Szabo explains how in pre-modern cultures, gifts created an implicit and widely acknowledged obligation in the recipient to reciprocate.

    https://nakamotoinstitute.org/shelling-out/

37. Graber, David. *Debt - Updated and Expanded: The First 5,000 Years*. Melville House, October 28, 2014, pp. 53.

    https://www.mhpbooks.com/books/debt/

38. Harford, Tim. "How the world's first accountants counted on cuneiform." *BBC World Service, 50 Things That Made the Modern Economy*, June 12, 2017.

    https://www.bbc.com/news/business-39870485

39. Supra note[36], Szabo quoting Richard Dawkins:

   "money is a formal token of delayed reciprocal altruism."

   Dawkins, Richard. *The Selfish Gene*, Oxford University Press, 1989.

   https://global.oup.com/academic/product/the-selfish-gene-978019
   8788607

40. Krawisz, Daniel. *Reciprocal Altruism in the Theory of Money*. Satoshi Nakamoto Institute, December 8, 2014.

   https://nakamotoinstitute.org/reciprocal-altruism-in-the-theory-o
   f-money/

41. Carroll, Lewis. *Alice's Adventures in Wonderland*. Macmillan, 1865.

42. Some authors use a lowercase 'b', bitcoin, to distinguish amounts of Bitcoin value from the computer network that secures the ledger. This book does not use the lowercase 'b' nomenclature. Rather, amounts of Bitcoin are written out as Bitcoin, ₿, or in terms of sats.

43. "Controlled Supply". *Bitcoin Wiki*, Retrieved March 10, 2020.

   https://en.bitcoin.it/wiki/Controlled_supply

44. GameKyuubi. *I AM HODLING*. Bitcoin Forum, December 18, 2013.

   https://bitcointalk.org/index.php?topic=375643.0

45. Maurer, Bill; Nelms, Taylor C.; and Swartz, Lana. "'When perhaps the real problem is money itself!': the practical materiality of Bitcoin." *Social Semiotics*, March 12, 2013.

   http://dx.doi.org/10.1080/10350330.2013.777594

46. Supra note[44].

47. Andolfatto, David and Spewak, Andrew. "Whither the Price of Bit-coin." *Economic Synopses*, Federal Reserve Bank of St. Louis, January 11, 2019.

    https://doi.org/10.20955/es.2019.1

48. Nakamoto, Satoshi. "Bitcoin open source implementation of P2P currency." P2P foundation, February 11, 2009.

    Comment on March 7, 2014: "I am not Dorian Nakamoto."

    http://p2pfoundation.ning.com/forum/topics/bitcoin-open-sourc e?commentId=2003008%3AComment%3A52186

49. Mayer, Trace. "The Seven Network Effects of Bitcoin." Talk hosted by CRYPSA at LaGuardia Community College, June 29, 2015.

    https://www.weusecoins.com/the-seven-network-effects-of-bit-coin/

50. "1994: 'Today Show': 'What is the Internet, Anyway?'" YouTube, Retrieved May 5, 2020.

    In this short clip, three Today Show hosts chat off-air, trying to fig-ure out what the Internet is. They are particularly confused about the '@' symbol in an email address, having never seen an email ad-dress before.

    https://youtu.be/UlJku_CSyNg

51. "Wordlists." bitcoin/bips repository on GitHub. Retrieved May 5, 2020.

    https://github.com/bitcoin/bips/blob/master/bip-0039/bip-0039-wordlists.md

52. Ferguson, Niels and Schneier, Bruce. *Practical Cryptography*. Wiley Publishing, Inc., 2003, pp. 326.

    https://www.schneier.com/books/practical_cryptography/

53. Abrams, Lawrence. "Clipboard Hijacker Malware Monitors 2.3 Million Bitcoin Addresses." Bleeping Computer, June 30, 2018.

    https://www.bleepingcomputer.com/news/security/clipboard-hijacker-malware-monitors-23-million-bitcoin-addresses/

54. Antonopoulos, Andreas M. *The Internet of Money* CreateSpace Independent Publishing Platform, August 30, 2016.

    https://theinternetofmoney.info/

55. "Glacier Protocol." Retrieved May 5, 2020.

    https://glacierprotocol.org/

56. "Good Delivery Explained." London Bullion Market Association (LBMA) website. Retrieved November 11, 2019.

    http://www.lbma.org.uk/good-delivery-explained

57. Singh, Manmohan and Aitken, James. "The (sizable) Role of Rehypothecation in the Shadow Banking System." International Monetary Fund, July 1, 2010.

    https://www.imf.org/external/pubs/ft/wp/2010/wp10172.pdf

58. Q.v. Chapter 1, Green Paper Bad, for more detail on the creation of bank account credit.

59. Gorton, Gary B. "Slapped in the Face by the Invisible Hand: Banking and the Panic of 2007." May 9, 2009.

    http://dx.doi.org/10.2139/ssrn.1401882

    Gorton argues that in the early 2000s, Mortgage Backed Securities had achieved money status in the shadow banking system by virtue of being informationally-insensitive debt instruments. The global financial crisis was then, in effect, a wholesale bank run caused by loss of faith in the money instrument (MSBs).

60. Q.v. Chapters 5-7 for more detail on how private keys secure your Bitcoin value.

61. Q.v. Chapter 7, Securing Your Bitcoin, for a brief explanation of multisig wallets.

62. "Timelock." *Bitcoin Wiki* Retrieved February 21, 2020.

    https://en.bitcoinwiki.org/wiki/Timelock

63. Pasha, Shaheen. "Government spying on your bank accounts." CNN Money, August 9, 2006.

    https://money.cnn.com/2006/08/09/news/economy/banks_secrecy/

64. Travis, Alan. "UK banks to check 70m bank accounts in search for illegal immigrants." *The Guardian*, September 21, 2017.

    https://www.theguardian.com/uk-news/2017/sep/21/uk-banks-to-check-70m-bank-accounts-in-search-for-illegal-immigrants

65. Q.v. Chapter 2, Because We Need Good Money.

66. Supra note[56] re Good Delivery.

67. Hobson, Peter. "Fake-branded bars slip dirty gold into world markets." Reuters, August 28, 2019.

    https://reut.rs/2LcfM8K

68. "The History of the Red Envelopes and How you can use them during the Year of the Yang Metal Rat 2020." Feng Shui Store website, Retrieved November 14, 2019.

    https://www.fengshuiweb.co.uk/advice/angpow.htm

69. "Money Stock and Debt Measures - H.6 Release." Board of Governors of the Federal Reserve System website, Retrieved November 14, 2019.

   o   October, 21 2019 M0: $1,693.8 billion.

   o   October, 21 2019 M2: $15,156.0 billion.

   o   M0 / M2 = 0.1118 (11.2%).

   https://www.federalreserve.gov/releases/h6/20191031/

70. Porter, Richard D. and Judson, Ruth A. "The Location of U.S. Currency:How Much Is Abroad?" Federal Reserve Bulletin, October 1996.

   https://www.federalreserve.gov/pubs/bulletin/1996/1096lead.pdf

71. Chang, Sue. "Here's all the money in the world, in one chart." MarketWatch website, November 28, 2017.

   o   Global Currency estimate (M0): $7.6 trillion.

   o   Broad Money estimate (M2): $90.4 trillion.

   o   M0 / M2 = 0.084 (8.4%).

   https://www.marketwatch.com/story/this-is-how-much-money-exists-in-the-entire-world-in-one-chart-2015-12-18

72. "Chargeback Rates. What is Normal and Why Does it Matter?" Chargebacks 911 website, Retrieved November, 14 2019.

   https://chargebacks911.com/chargeback-rate/

73. Putting aside radioactive gold atomic isotopes.

74. U.S. Department of the Treasury. "Cyber-related Designations; Publication of New Cyber-related FAQs." U.S. Treasury website, November 28, 2018.

   https://www.treasury.gov/resource-center/sanctions/OFAC-Enforcement/Pages/20181128.aspx

75. U.S. Department of the Treasury. "Treasury Designates Iran-Based Financial Facilitators of Malicious Cyber Activity and for the First Time Identifies Associated Digital Currency Addresses." U.S. Treasury website, November 28, 2018.

https://home.treasury.gov/news/press-releases/sm556

76. Schoenberg, Tom and Robinson, Matt. "Lotto Beer Bitcoin." *Bloomberg Businessweek*, December 17, 2018.

https://www.bloomberg.com/features/2018-bitcoin-atm-money-laundering/

77. Alexandre, Ana. "Brazilian Police Arrest Suspect for Money Laundering With Bitcoin." Cointelegraph, April 24, 2019.

https://cointelegraph.com/news/brazilian-police-arrest-suspect-for-money-laundering-with-bitcoin

78. Maxwell, Gregory. "CoinJoin: Bitcoin privacy for the real world." *Bitcoin Forum*, August 22, 2013.

https://bitcointalk.org/?topic=279249

79. *bitcoin/bips*, Accessed October 12, 2020.

Bitcoin Improvement Proposals (BIPs) are descriptions of potential changes to Bitcoin. See BIPs 340, 341 and 342 by Wuille et al. for details on Schnorr and Taproot activation.

https://github.com/bitcoin/bips/

80. Ammous, Saifedean. *The Bitcoin Standard: The Decentralized Alternative to Central Banking*. John Wiley & Sons, April, 2018.

https://www.wiley.com/en-us/The+Bitcoin+Standard%3A+The+Decentralized+Alternative+to+Central+Banking-p-9781119473862

81. Supra note[36].

82. Computing the 2018 gold stock increase based on [95][96]:

    o (2018 increase) / (2019 total - 2019 increase)

    o 3260 / (193,500 - 3260) = 0.01714 = 1.7%

83. "16 Psyche." NASA Science, Solar System Exploration, May 9, 2019.

    https://solarsystem.nasa.gov/asteroids-comets-and-meteors/asteroids/16-psyche/in-depth/

84. Murphy, Margi. "SPACE GOLD RUSH Nasa announces 2022 mission to explore metal asteroid so valuable it could crash the world economy." *The Sun*, May 25, 2017.

    https://www.thesun.co.uk/tech/3646967/nasa-reveals-launch-date-of-mission-to-explore-metal-asteroid-so-valuable-it-would-crash-the-world-economy/

85. Stringham, Edward Peter. "Economic Value and Cost are Subjective." *Handbook on Contemporary Austrian Economics*, Peter J. Boettke, ed., Edward Elgar Publishing, September 13, 2010.

    https://ssrn.com/abstract=1676261

86. Here I'm using the term 'liability' according to Kiyosaki's categorization:

    o Commodities are things you use up.

    o Liabilities are things that take money out of your pocket.

    o Assets are things that put money into your pocket.

    Kiyosaki, Robert T. *Rich Dad Poor Dad: What the Rich Teach Their Kids About Money That the Poor and Middle Class Do Not!* Plata Publishing, 2017.

    https://www.amazon.com/gp/product/1612680194

87. Bronstein, Hugh and Raszewski, Eliana. "How Argentina's youth learned to worry about the peso and love the dollar." Reuters, December 2, 2019.

https://reut.rs/2qTj76x

88. Burgos, Jonathan and Ismail, Netty. "New York Apartments, Art Top Gold as Stores of Wealth, Says Fink." Bloomberg, April 21, 2015.

https://www.bloomberg.com/news/articles/2015-04-21/new-york-apartments-art-top-gold-as-stores-of-wealth-says-fink

89. Markowitz, Harry. "Portfolio Selection." *The Journal of Finance*, vol. 7, no. 1, 1952, pp. 77–91. doi:10.2307/2975974

https://www.jstor.org/stable/2975974

90. Chen, James. "Risk-Free Rate of Return." *Investopedia*, Updated October 1, 2019.

https://www.investopedia.com/terms/r/risk-freerate.asp

91. Tymoigne, Éric and Wray, L. Randall. "Modern Money Theory 101: A Reply to Critics." Levy Economics Institute of Bard College, November, 2013, pp. 5.

http://www.levyinstitute.org/pubs/wp_778.pdf

92. Supra note[89].

93. Sharpe, W. F. "Mutual Fund Performance." *Journal of Business*, vol. 39, no. 1, 1966, pp. 119–138. doi:10.1086/294846.

https://doi.org/10.1086/294846

94. Anadu, Kenechukwu; Kruttli, Mathias S.; McCabe, Patrick E.; Osam-
bela, Emilio; and Shin, Chaehee. "The Shift From Active to Passive
Investing: Potential Risks to Financial Stability?" December 17,
2019. doi:10.2139/ssrn.3244467

https://ssrn.com/abstract=3244467

95. "Mineral Commodity Summaries 2019." USGS website, Retrieved
May 5, 2020.

o   World total mine production 2018: 3260 tons.

https://www.usgs.gov/centers/nmic/mineral-commodity-sum-
maries

96. "Above-ground stocks." Gold Hub website, January 31, 2019.

o   World total above ground gold 2019 estimate: 193,500 tonnes.

https://www.gold.org/goldhub/data/above-ground-stocks

www.ingramcontent.com/pod-product-compliance
Lightning Source LLC
Chambersburg PA
CBHW071249050326
40690CB00011B/2324